Y0-DND-604

Evaluation of the

MINERVA RESEARCH INITIATIVE

Committee to Assess the Minerva Research
Initiative and the Contribution of Social Science to
Addressing Security Concerns

Allen L. Schirm, Krisztina Marton, and Jeanne C. Rivard, *Editors*

Board on Behavioral, Cognitive, and Sensory Sciences

Division of Behavioral and Social Sciences and Education

A Consensus Study Report of

The National Academies of
SCIENCES · ENGINEERING · MEDICINE

THE NATIONAL ACADEMIES PRESS
Washington, DC
www.nap.edu

THE NATIONAL ACADEMIES PRESS   500 Fifth Street, NW   Washington, DC 20001

This activity was supported by contracts between the National Academy of Sciences and the Department of Defense (#W911NF-13-D-0002, DO #4). Support for the work of the Board on Behavioral, Cognitive, and Sensory Sciences is provided primarily by a grant from the National Science Foundation (Award No. BCS-1729167). Any opinions, findings, conclusions, or recommendations expressed in this publication do not necessarily reflect the views of any organization or agency that provided support for the project.

International Standard Book Number-13: 978-0-309-49428-1
International Standard Book Number-10: 0-309-49428-1
Digital Object Identifier: https://doi.org/10.17226/25482

Additional copies of this publication are available from the National Academies Press, 500 Fifth Street, NW, Keck 360, Washington, DC 20001; (800) 624-6242 or (202) 334-3313; http://www.nap.edu.

Copyright 2020 by the National Academy of Sciences. All rights reserved.

Printed in the United States of America

Suggested citation: National Academies of Sciences, Engineering, and Medicine. 2020. *Evaluation of the Minerva Research Initiative*. Washington, DC: The National Academies Press. https://doi.org/10.17226/25482.

The National Academies of
SCIENCES • ENGINEERING • MEDICINE

The **National Academy of Sciences** was established in 1863 by an Act of Congress, signed by President Lincoln, as a private, nongovernmental institution to advise the nation on issues related to science and technology. Members are elected by their peers for outstanding contributions to research. Dr. Marcia McNutt is president.

The **National Academy of Engineering** was established in 1964 under the charter of the National Academy of Sciences to bring the practices of engineering to advising the nation. Members are elected by their peers for extraordinary contributions to engineering. Dr. John L. Anderson is president.

The **National Academy of Medicine** (formerly the Institute of Medicine) was established in 1970 under the charter of the National Academy of Sciences to advise the nation on medical and health issues. Members are elected by their peers for distinguished contributions to medicine and health. Dr. Victor J. Dzau is president.

The three Academies work together as the **National Academies of Sciences, Engineering, and Medicine** to provide independent, objective analysis and advice to the nation and conduct other activities to solve complex problems and inform public policy decisions. The National Academies also encourage education and research, recognize outstanding contributions to knowledge, and increase public understanding in matters of science, engineering, and medicine.

Learn more about the National Academies of Sciences, Engineering, and Medicine at **www.nationalacademies.org**.

The National Academies of
SCIENCES · ENGINEERING · MEDICINE

Consensus Study Reports published by the National Academies of Sciences, Engineering, and Medicine document the evidence-based consensus on the study's statement of task by an authoring committee of experts. Reports typically include findings, conclusions, and recommendations based on information gathered by the committee and the committee's deliberations. Each report has been subjected to a rigorous and independent peer-review process and it represents the position of the National Academies on the statement of task.

Proceedings published by the National Academies of Sciences, Engineering, and Medicine chronicle the presentations and discussions at a workshop, symposium, or other event convened by the National Academies. The statements and opinions contained in proceedings are those of the participants and are not endorsed by other participants, the planning committee, or the National Academies.

For information about other products and activities of the National Academies, please visit www.nationalacademies.org/about/whatwedo.

COMMITTEE TO ASSESS THE MINERVA RESEARCH INITIATIVE AND THE CONTRIBUTION OF SOCIAL SCIENCE TO ADDRESSING SECURITY CONCERNS

ALLEN L. SCHIRM (*Chair*), Mathematica Policy Research (retired)
BURT S. BARNOW, The George Washington University
KAREN S. COOK, Stanford University
SUSAN E. COZZENS, Georgia Institute of Technology
BARBARA ENTWISLE, University of North Carolina at Chapel Hill
IVY ESTABROOKE, PolarityTE, Inc.
PAUL A. GADE, U.S. Army Research Institute for the Behavioral and Social Sciences (retired)
ROBERT M. HAUSER, American Philosophical Society
STEVEN G. HEERINGA, University of Michigan Institute for Social Research
DANIEL R. ILGEN, Michigan State University
VIRGINIA LESSER, Oregon State University
ARTHUR LUPIA, University of Michigan*
KATHRYN E. NEWCOMER, The George Washington University
MARK L. WEISS, National Science Foundation (retired)

KRISZTINA MARTON, Study Director
JEANNE C. RIVARD, Senior Program Officer
ANTHONY MANN, Program Associate
ADRIENNE STITH BUTLER, Associate Board Director

*Resigned from the committee effective September 1, 2018.

BOARD ON BEHAVIORAL, COGNITIVE, AND SENSORY SCIENCES

SUSAN FISKE (*Chair*), Eugene Higgins Professor, Psychology and Public Affairs, Princeton University
JOHN BAUGH, Margaret Bush Wilson Professor, Linguistics, Washington University, St. Louis
LAURA CARSTENSEN, Fairleigh S. Dickinson Jr. Professor, Public Policy, Department of Psychology, Stanford University
JUDY DUBNO, Professor, Medical University of South Carolina
JENNIFER EBERHARDT, Director and Research Professor, Institute for Social Research, Stanford University
WILSON S. GEISLER, David Wechsler Professor of Psychology and Director, Center for Perceptual Systems, The University of Texas
MICHELLE GELFAND, Professor of Psychology and Distinguished University Professor, University of Maryland
NANCY G. KANWISHER, Professor, Department of Brain and Cognitive Sciences, McGovern Institute for Brain Research, Massachusetts Institute of Technology
JANICE KIECOLT-GLASER, Distinguished University Professor, S. Robert Davis Chair of Medicine, and Professor of Psychiatry and Psychology, Institute for Behavioral Medicine Research, Ohio State University College of Medicine
WILLIAM (BILL) MAUER, Professor of Anthropology, Law and Criminology, and Law and Society; Dean, School of Social Sciences; and Director, Institute for Money, Technology and Financial Inclusion, University of California, Irvine
TERRIE E. MOFFITT, Professor of Psychology and Neuroscience, Duke University
ELIZABETH A. PHELPS, Pershing Square Professor of Human Neuroscience, Department of Psychology, Harvard University
STEVEN E. PETERSEN, James S. McDonnell Professor of Cognitive Neuroscience in Neurology, Washington University
DANA SMALL, Professor and Deputy Director, Yale University
TIMOTHY J. STRAUMAN, Professor, Duke University

BARBARA A. WANCHISEN, Board Director

Acknowledgments

On behalf of the Committee to Assess the Minerva Research Initiative and the Contribution of Social Science to Addressing Security Concerns, we thank the many people who contributed their time and expertise to assist in the committee's work and the preparation of this report. The study was initiated by the Department of Defense (DoD), under the leadership of then–director of the Basic Research Office, Robin Staffin, and Minerva Research Initiative interim director Lisa Troyer, and has greatly benefited from the input and continued support of DoD's senior management. We are particularly grateful to Minerva Research Initiative director, David Montgomery, for facilitating the work of the committee.

DoD staff readily assisted the committee through presentations and responses to a large number of requests for background materials about the Minerva Research Initiative. We thank not only David Montgomery and Lisa Troyer, but also Bindu Nair, Kaleb Redden, Benjamin Knott, Gary Kollmorgen, and Martin Kruger.

The committee is grateful for the input provided during our public sessions by Minerva grantees, national security experts, representatives of social science organizations, and staff from other government agencies, including (but not limited to) those who are named in Appendix G of the report. Special appreciation is extended to current and former DoD personnel, principal investigators of Minerva grants, and staff of academic offices of sponsored research who shared their valuable time by participating in interviews and surveys conducted by the committee for this evaluation. The committee also thanks Diana Hicks, Georgia Institute of Technology, for expert consultation on methods for evaluating research outputs.

This Consensus Study Report was reviewed in draft form by individuals chosen for their diverse perspectives and technical expertise. The purpose of this independent review is to provide candid and critical comments that will assist the National Academies of Sciences, Engineering, and Medicine in making each published report as sound as possible and to ensure that it meets the institutional standards for quality, objectivity, evidence, and responsiveness to the study charge. The review comments and draft manuscript remain confidential to protect the integrity of the deliberative process.

We thank the following individuals for their review of this report: Myron P. Gutmann, Institute of Behavioral Science, University of Colorado, Boulder; Brian Nosek, Center for Open Science, University of Virginia; Sarah M. Nusser, Center for Survey Statistics and Methodology, Iowa State University; Joy Rohde, Ford School of Public Policy, University of Michigan; C. Matthew Snipp, Department of Sociology and Stanford Secure Data Center, Stanford University; Robert J. Ursano, Center for the Study of Traumatic Stress and Department of Psychiatry, Uniformed Services University of the Health Sciences; and Alyson Wilson, Department of Statistics, North Carolina State University.

Although the reviewers listed above provided many constructive comments and suggestions, they were not asked to endorse the conclusions or recommendations of this report nor did they see the final draft before its release. The review of this report was overseen by report review coordinator Jonathan D. Moreno, Department of Medical Ethics and Health Policy, University of Pennsylvania Health System and report review monitor Anita K. Jones, School of Engineering, University of Virginia. They were responsible for making certain that an independent examination of this report was carried out in accordance with the standards of the National Academies and that all review comments were carefully considered. Responsibility for the final content rests entirely with the authoring committee and the National Academies.

Finally, we thank the National Research Council staff who contributed to this study. We are grateful for the guidance and support received from Barbara Wanchisen, director of the Board on Behavioral, Cognitive, and Sensory Sciences (BBCSS); Adrienne Stith Butler, deputy director of BBCSS; Jeanne Rivard, senior program officer; Constance Citro, senior scholar with the Committee on National Statistics; and Brian Harris-Kojetin, director of the Committee on National Statistics. Kirsten Sampson Snyder expertly coordinated the review process, and Rona Briere provided thoughtful editorial help. We thank program associate Anthony Mann for his good humor and many skills in providing logistical support for the committee's meetings. We also thank the staff of the National Academies' Research Center Library, Colleen Willis and Christopher Lao-Scott, for research support and assistance with the use of library resources during the evaluation. To conclude these acknowledgments, Allen would like to thank Krisztina for her exceptional contributions as study director. The evaluation would have been far less successful without her hard work and tremendous management and research skills. Collaborating on this study with Krisztina was a pleasure.

Allen L. Schirm, *Chair*
Krisztina Marton, *Study Director*

Acronyms

AAA	American Anthropological Association
AFOSR	Air Force Office of Scientific Research
ARO	Army Research Office
ASD R&E	Assistant Secretary of Defense for Research and Engineering
BAA	Broad Agency Announcement (for funding)
BRO	Basic Research Office
DHS	Department of Homeland Security
DoD	Department of Defense
FOA	Funding Opportunity Announcement
IRB	Institutional Review Board
MOU	Memorandum of Understanding
MRI	Minerva Research Initiative
NORC	National Opinion Research Center
NSF	National Science Foundation
ONR	Office of Naval Research
OSD	Office of the Secretary of Defense
OUSD	Office of the Under Secretary of Defense
OUSD-Policy	Office of the Under Secretary of Defense for Policy

OUSD-R&E	Office of the Under Secretary of Defense for Research and Engineering
SJR	Scimago Journal Ranking

Contents

SUMMARY   1

1 INTRODUCTION   7
History of the Minerva Research Initiative and Context
   for the Study, 7
Charge to the Committee, 18

**2 OVERVIEW OF THE COMMITTEE'S
INFORMATION-GATHERING ACTIVITIES**   27
Reviews of Department of Defense and Other Public Records, 27
Interviews with Department of Defense Staff, 32
Grantee Survey, 33
Survey of Administrators of Sponsored Research at
   Academic Institutions, 38
Minerva Conference, 40
Public Information-Gathering Sessions, 40
Limitations of the Committee's Evaluation, 40

3 PROCESSES OF THE MINERVA PROGRAM   43
Overview of Program Processes, 44
Discussion of Minerva Program Processes, 52

4	**RESEARCH SUPPORTED BY THE MINERVA PROGRAM: QUANTITY AND QUALITY**	61
	Review of Outputs of the Minerva Research Initiative Grants, 61	
	Stakeholder and Expert Perceptions of the Quality of Minerva Research, 74	
	Summary and Conclusions, 77	
5	**DIRECTION AND VISION OF THE MINERVA PROGRAM**	79
	Making Better Use of Minerva Research and Researchers, 79	
	Discussion of Minerva's Vision and Goals, 86	
	Increasing Social Scientists' Engagement with the Program, 87	
	Developing Benchmarks for Continuous Monitoring and Evaluation, 92	

REFERENCES 93

APPENDIXES

A-1	2017 Preliminary Federal Obligations for Basic Research, by Agency and Field of Science and Engineering (dollars in thousands)	97
A-2	2016 Federal Obligations for Basic Research Performed at Universities and Colleges in Social Sciences, by Selected Agency and Detailed Field (dollars in thousands)	102
B	Minerva Research Topics in Grant Announcements Issued between 2008 and 2018	103
C	List of Minerva Grant Awards between 2009 and 2017	109
D	Interview Protocol for Individual Interviews with Current and Former Minerva Research Initiative Staff	119
E	Survey of Minerva Grantees	123
F	Survey of Administrators of Sponsored Research	135
G	Individuals Who Provided Input during the Committee's Public Meetings	145
H	Output Categories and Coding Notes	147
I	Publications and Presentations by Year (rounded to nearest whole number)	149
J-1	Impact Metrics of Journals in Which Minerva Principal Investigators Reported Publishing	151
J-2	Journals without Journal-Level Impact Factor Scores in Which Minerva Principal Investigators Published	160

K	Field-Weighted Citation Impact of Publications Reported by Principal Investigators	161
L	Universities with Minerva Grants: Classification of Research Institution Type Based on Carnegie Classification of Institutions of Higher Education	169
M	Biographical Sketches of Committee Members and Staff	175

Summary

The Minerva Research Initiative is a social science research grant program that funds academic scientists to conduct unclassified basic research relevant to national security issues. Launched in 2008 by Secretary of Defense Robert Gates, the program was motivated by the recognition that the Department of Defense (DoD) was making insufficient use of the intellectual capital of university-based social scientists, as well as a desire to revitalize the role of social science research in informing understanding of the "social, cultural, behavioral, and political forces that shape regions of the world of strategic importance to the U.S." within DoD and the broader national security community (Minerva Research Initiative, n.d.).

In 2017, DoD asked the National Academies of Sciences, Engineering, and Medicine to convene a committee to evaluate the program's successes and challenges during its first decade of operation and to offer guidance on its best path going forward. To this end, the committee reviewed existing documentation on the program and its grants, conducted two surveys and a series of semistructured interviews, attended the 2018 Minerva Meeting and Program Review, met with a broad range of stakeholders, and issued a request for comments. As a result of these activities, the committee was able to gain an in-depth understanding of the program from diverse perspectives.

The committee's review of Minerva's accomplishments to date revealed that, despite facing challenges with establishing a stable, well-functioning organizational structure as well as resource limitations, the program has made important contributions. The Minerva program is competitive, and funds unclassified basic research on broadly defined topics, enabling the researchers of the awarded grants to pursue questions and analyses they consider important and to produce research that is relevant to both national security and social science more generally. Over the years, Minerva research has been published in top journals and tends to have strong citation records. The research has also resulted in books and produced policy-relevant statistical models, databases, and mapping tools, reflecting the value placed by the program on innovative outputs beyond publications and conference presentations.

Many of the projects have been built on interdisciplinary collaborations that have incorporated perspectives from a variety of social and behavioral sciences, as well as other fields, such as computer science and engineering. Minerva research has been published in journals representing all major social science fields, as well as other fields (such as computer science, engineering, and mathematics), further illustrating the program's reach and the range of disciplines that are brought together by the program to answer research questions. Grantees reported that the program has had a positive impact on the amount of dialogue between DoD and the social science community, the number of social science researchers with an interest in research relevant to national security, and the amount of collaboration among researchers working on topics relevant to national security.

We note that the committee's statement of task included an assessment of Minerva's quality and impact. Measuring quality and estimating impact, however, are difficult in the context of evaluating programs like Minerva. Measuring the quality of a research product (or a researcher) is conceptually and practically challenging, and the available metrics have substantial limitations, making their use controversial. Estimating Minerva's impacts is even more difficult because a rigorous approach to evaluating a program's causal effects requires an analysis of the "counterfactual," that is, estimation of what would have happened in the absence of the program. The committee determined that the available data were not adequate for this purpose. Furthermore, given that some of Minerva's key outcomes—such as the contribution and influence of research and the creation of research communities—are realized over a long period of time, it would generally take many years to allow research to be conducted, key outcomes to be observed, and new data to be collected for both a research group with Minerva funding and an experimental or other valid comparison group without Minerva funding (the counterfactual).[1] Consequently, the

---

[1] The gold standard approach to evaluating causal impact is a randomized controlled trial, although other statistical designs and methods can sometimes be used to control for confounding and enable a program's effects to be isolated from other influences. However, the committee determined that implementation of such an approach and collection of data to support credible inferences about Minerva's impacts could not be accomplished for this evaluation, certainly not within the timeframe for providing useful guidance to DoD.

committee's ability to answer some of the questions in the statement of task was limited.

It is clear that the vision and goals of the program still resonate in the national security community and among academic researchers, and this report offers the committee's recommendations for building on that vision to strengthen the program going forward. The report's key messages and main recommendations are grouped into a thematic summary below.

The Minerva program was structured as a collaboration between research and policy divisions within DoD, and one of the challenges it has faced has been balancing the funding priorities emerging from their differing perspectives and priorities. In particular, DoD has struggled with defining the role of the military service branches (the Air Force Office of Scientific Research, the Army Research Office, and the Office of Naval Research) in the management of the program. Changes introduced in 2017 (around the time the committee undertook this study) increased the role of the service branches in all aspects of decision making related to the Minerva program. While it is too early to assess how the restructured program will function, a key task for DoD is to define the program's priorities more clearly and make decisions going forward with these priorities in mind.

> **RECOMMENDATION 5.6:** The Minerva program office should specify its priorities for the Minerva Research Initiative, and, as needed, refine the program's approach to topic selection and grant award to reflect these priorities.

In recent years, the Minerva program has also experienced challenges associated with staff turnover. Successfully implementing the recommendations offered in this report will depend on ensuring stable staffing of the Minerva program office.

> **RECOMMENDATION 3.1:** The Department of Defense should ensure that the Minerva Research Initiative has a leader with appropriate credentials and stature in a full-time, civil service position.

> **RECOMMENDATION 3.2:** The Department of Defense should evaluate what additional support staff are needed for the Minerva Research Initiative to achieve its goals and implement the recommendations in this report.

The best opportunities for making better use of the program's research and the expertise of its researchers lie in outreach and dissemination. Increased outreach and dissemination are needed to exploit opportunities for Minerva-funded research to inform the policy discourse, and to expand the communities that can benefit from the body of knowledge generated through the Minerva grants, as well as from the expertise of the funded researchers.

> RECOMMENDATION 5.1: The Minerva program office should develop a strategic outreach and dissemination plan for distributing information about the Minerva Research Initiative and about the studies and researchers funded.

The development of a centralized database of all Minerva grants awarded to date should be the highest-priority task for the Minerva program office, as a foundation for dissemination activities.

> RECOMMENDATION 3.3: The Minerva program office should make completing the centralized database of the projects and researchers funded under the Minerva Research Initiative a high priority.

> RECOMMENDATION 5.2: The public-facing component of the grantee database to be developed by the Minerva program office should include detailed information about the funded projects, providing a current and historical picture of the portfolio of research that has been conducted and an inventory of the researchers' expertise. The database should be user-friendly and searchable.

Several areas need particular attention as part of a comprehensive outreach and dissemination strategy. Awareness of the Minerva program needs to be increased both internally, within DoD, and in the broader national security community. In addition, grantees would greatly benefit from the Minerva program office's assistance in creating opportunities for interaction with policy makers and others who could benefit from their research and their broader expertise.

> RECOMMENDATION 3.4: The Minerva program office should develop relationships with potential supporters of the Minerva Research Initiative and users of the research, both among Department of Defense leadership and externally, to increase awareness of the program and expand use of its funded research and the expertise of its grantees.

> RECOMMENDATION 5.3: The Minerva program office should develop mechanisms for facilitating interaction between grantees and potential users of their research or expertise in the broader national security community.

RECOMMENDATION 5.5: The Minerva Conference should continue to serve as a key mechanism for outreach, dissemination, and interaction and should be held annually, on a predictable schedule.

The committee's overall assessment is that during its first decade, the Minerva program has demonstrated its ability to make meaningful contributions to the body of social science research on a range of topics related to national security. Considering the program's original vision and continuing goals, the committee's recommendations highlight areas in which the Minerva program office needs to focus its efforts to strengthen the program's foundations and take advantage of opportunities for broadening its reach and usefulness going forward.

1

Introduction

The Minerva Research Initiative is a Department of Defense (DoD) grant program whose vision is to "support social science research for a safer world" (Minerva Research Initiative, n.d.). The program funds unclassified academic social science research "aimed at improving our basic understanding of security, broadly defined." As described further below, the program is a collaboration across several DoD units, designed to bring together leadership from different divisions to "identify and support basic social science research issues in need of attention and to integrate those research insights into the policy-making environment" (Minerva Research Initiative, n.d.). Box 1-1 summarizes the program's objectives.

HISTORY OF THE MINERVA RESEARCH INITIATIVE AND CONTEXT FOR THE STUDY

Origins of the Program

The Minerva Research Initiative was launched in 2008 by Secretary of Defense Robert Gates, motivated by the recognition that DoD was underutilizing the intellectual capital of university-based social scientists, as well as a desire to revitalize the role of social science research in informing understanding of the "social, cultural, behavioral, and political forces that shape regions of the world of strategic importance to the U.S." (Minerva Research Initiative, n.d.) within DoD and the broader research community. In a speech, Gates urged, "we must again embrace eggheads and ideas" (Department of Defense, 2008).

> **BOX 1-1**
> **Objectives of the Minerva Research Initiative**
>
> The goal of the Minerva Initiative is to improve DoD's basic understanding of the social, cultural, behavioral, and political forces that shape regions of the world of strategic importance to the U.S.
> The research program will:
>
> - Leverage and focus the resources of the Nation's top universities.
> - Seek to define and develop foundational knowledge about sources of present and future conflict with an eye toward better understanding of the political trajectories of key regions of the world.
> - Improve the ability of DoD to develop cutting-edge social science research, foreign area and interdisciplinary studies, that is developed and vetted by the best scholars in these fields.
>
> The Minerva Initiative brings together universities, research institutions, and individual scholars and supports interdisciplinary and cross-institutional projects addressing specific topic areas determined by the Secretary of Defense.
>
> SOURCE: Excerpted from Minerva Research Initiative (n.d.).

There had been collaborations between DoD and academic social science researchers in the decades prior to the launch of the Minerva program, particularly during the Cold War, but these efforts had often been controversial because of concerns raised about the potential militarization of research and skepticism about whether the scholarship would be responsive to national security needs. After the September 11, 2001, attacks, interest in utilizing insights from social science research in the realm of national security reemerged.

In a speech delivered at a meeting of the Association of American Universities in 2008, Secretary Gates elaborated on his thoughts and intentions with respect to the Minerva program:

> Let me be clear that the key principle of all components of the Minerva Consortia will be complete openness and rigid adherence to academic freedom and integrity. There will be no room for "sensitive but unclassified," or other such restrictions in this project. We are interested in furthering our knowledge of these issues and in soliciting diverse points of view—regardless of whether those views are critical of the Department's efforts. Too many mistakes have been made over the years because our government and military did not understand—or even seek to understand—the countries or cultures we were dealing with. (Department of Defense, 2008)

Secretary Gates' speech did not entirely ease all concerns among social scientists, however (for some position papers, see http://essays.ssrc.org/minerva; also see National Academies of Sciences, Engineering, and Medicine, 2019a). In 2008, for example, the American Anthropological Association (AAA), representing academics in the discipline that had been at the center of the prior controversies related to collaborations with DoD, issued a letter addressed to the Office of Management and Budget. In this letter, the AAA argued that funding for Minerva grants should be routed through an agency such as the National Science Foundation (NSF), the National Institutes of Health, or the National Endowment for the Humanities because of these agencies' longer histories, relative to DoD, with funding academic research based on a well-established peer review system (Low, 2008). The AAA argued that DoD would be unable to develop a review process that would ensure the funding of rigorous academic research.

To address such concerns, DoD signed a memorandum of understanding (MOU) with NSF in 2008 "to support high-quality basic research in the social and behavioral sciences that has the potential for beneficial application and use in military contexts." According to this MOU, "coordination between the agencies will include the development of solicitations and a management plan for the competition, cooperation in the selection of reviewers and advisory panel members, and cooperation in the selection of proposals to be awarded" (National Science Foundation and Department of Defense, 2008). As part of the collaboration between DoD and NSF, 18 grants were funded in 2010. Simultaneously with its negotiations with NSF, DoD also began awarding grants on a separate track. The collaboration with NSF ended after the initial round of grants because the two agencies' differing approaches to awarding and managing grants proved too challenging to combine into one program.

In the program's first year (2008), only one large grant was funded, focused on addressing an existing need related to terrorism. In 2009, only a small number of projects were funded, in part because the goal was to fund just a few large consortia. Starting in 2010, DoD began issuing Broad Agency Announcements (later referred to as Funding Opportunity Announcements) on grants.gov, and awareness of the program gradually increased. Grant announcements are now typically issued on an annual cycle.

Consistent with its original focus on unclassified research and scientific merit, the Minerva program is open to researchers of any nationality. Funds are awarded to the researcher's academic institution, which must be a university either in the United States or abroad; thus, independent researchers not affiliated with an academic institution are ineligible. Because the program emphasizes capacity building and interdisciplinary research, grants are often awarded to teams of researchers, but single-investigator proposals are also eligible for consideration. Over the years, the emphasis has shifted from very large consortia to midsized grants.

The program's proposal process consists of two stages. In the first stage, researchers are encouraged (but not required) to submit a short version of their proposal (referred to as a white paper). Researchers whose white papers are deemed most competitive then receive an invitation to submit a full proposal.

Characteristics of the Program

Within DoD, the Minerva Research Initiative is managed by the Basic Research Office (BRO) in the Office of the Under Secretary of Defense for Research and Engineering (OUSD-R&E) in partnership with the Office of the Deputy Assistant Secretary of Defense for Strategy and Force Development in the Office of the Under Secretary of Defense for Policy (OUSD-Policy) and the military service branches. The program's grants are executed by and receive technical oversight from program managers from the basic research units of the service branches: the Air Force Office of Scientific Research (AFOSR), the Army Research Office (ARO), and the Office of Naval Research (ONR). Figure 1-1 shows the distribution of Minerva funds by source of funding. The investment in the program has been around $20–$22 million annually, with the BRO within OUSD-R&E contributing the majority of the funds. In 2016, Congress allocated additional funds to

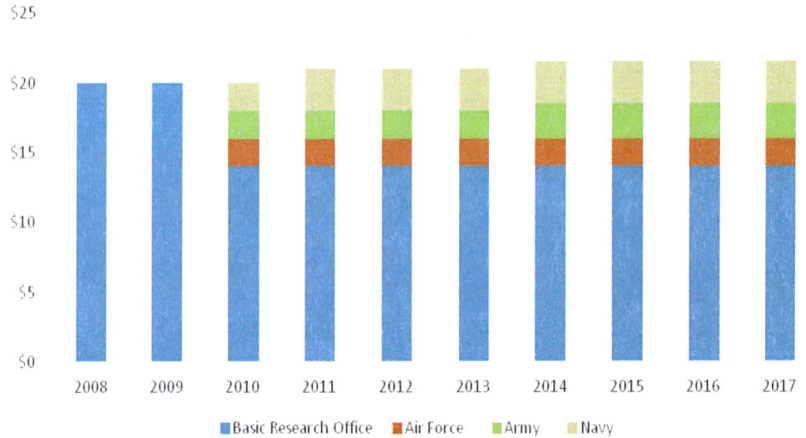

FIGURE 1-1 Minerva funding by source, in millions of dollars.
NOTE: In 2016 the Basic Research Office received additional funds from Congress and was able to contribute an additional $10 million to the Minerva program. This brought the total for that year to $32 million.
SOURCE: Nair (2018).

INTRODUCTION

BRO, and $10 million was used to increase funding for the Minerva program. The three service branches together have typically contributed about one-third of the funds. As of October 2018, ARO decided to withdraw from the partnership and to no longer support new awards starting with fiscal year 2019. The reasons for its withdrawal are briefly described below and discussed in further detail in Chapter 3.

Using data compiled regularly by NSF, Appendix A-1 shows federal obligations for social science research, by agency and field, while Appendix A-2 shows federal obligations for basic social science research performed at academic institutions, by agency and field. DoD was unable to confirm how the Minerva funding is reported to NSF by the service branches. The service branches have their own basic research programs, and the structure of these programs does not necessarily overlap with how NSF collects the data, which likely means that there are inconsistencies in reporting. These data are not sufficient to compare the Minerva program's size with that of other, similar programs without making assumptions, but the program's focus on funding academic researchers to conduct unclassified basic social science research on issues relevant to national security means that Minerva has a unique role in the funding landscape for social science research.

Figure 1-2 shows how Minerva basic research projects fit within the classification of scientific research proposed by Stokes (1997, Ch. 1). While some projects pursue basic research aimed exclusively at greater fundamental

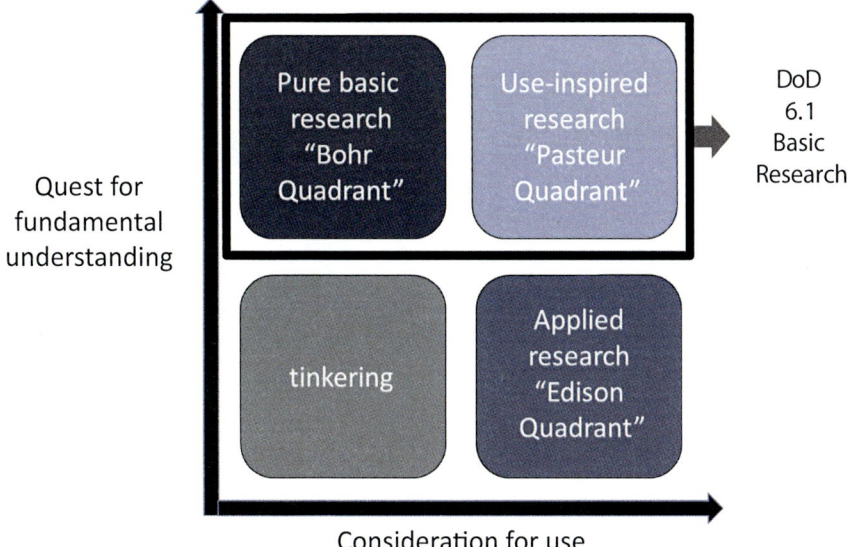

FIGURE 1-2 Classification of Minerva-funded research.
SOURCE: Adapted from Stokes (1997).

understanding (and fall into the "Bohr quadrant" in Stokes' framework), other projects are inspired by both the search for greater understanding and potential uses of the research (and fall into the "Pasteur quadrant").

The Minerva program's structure was designed to bring together DoD staff who can contribute different perspectives: research staff focused on the scientific merit of the grants (the BRO staff in OUSD-R&E and typically the service branch program managers) and policy staff focused on the policy relevance of the work (OUSD-Policy staff). There was also a practical need to utilize the contracting and project management capabilities of the service branches to administer the grants because OUSD cannot issue grants.

The committee's interviews with DoD staff made it clear, however, that reconciling priorities across these different entities resulted in some challenges over the years with respect to funding priorities. Prior to 2017, the topics and projects to be funded were selected by OUSD-Policy in partnership with OUSD-R&E. The service branch program managers had only minor input into this part of the process, and were assigned topics and specific grants to manage on behalf of the program. This arrangement led to some discontent among the service branches, in part because the topics and methodological approaches valued in basic research are often not the ones that are clearly associated with immediate policy implications.

DoD has worked to address these challenges, and as of 2017 had expanded the role of the service branches to include all aspects of the program. Table 1-1 summarizes the changes implemented. Now, topics are initially proposed by the service branch program managers, who work with the Minerva director to ensure that Office of the Secretary of

TABLE 1-1 Comparison of the Roles of the Office of the Secretary of Defense (OSD) and the Military Service Branches Before and After 2017

Process	Before 2017 OSD	Before 2017 Military Service Branches	2017 and After OSD	2017 and After Military Service Branches
Topic Selection	✓		✓	✓
White Paper Review Process	✓	✓		✓
Proposal Invite	✓			✓
Proposal Review Process	✓	✓	✓	✓
Proposal Selection	✓		✓	✓
Project Management		✓		✓
Grant Cycle Management	✓		✓	✓

SOURCE: Montgomery (2019).

> **BOX 1-2**
> **Topics from the 2018 Minerva Funding Opportunity Announcement**
>
> Topic 1: Sociopolitical (In)Stability, Resilience, and Recovery
> Topic 2: Economic Interdependence and Security
> Topic 3: Alliances and Burden Sharing
> Topic 4: Fundamental Dynamics of Scientific Discovery
> Topic 5: Adversarial Information Campaigns
> Topic 6: Automated Cyber Vulnerability Analysis
> Topic 7: Power, Deterrence, Influence, and Escalation Management for Shaping Operations
> Topic 8: Security Risks in Ungoverned & Semi-Governed Spaces*
>
> SOURCE: Department of Defense Washington Headquarters Services/Acquisition Directorate, 2018.
>
> *Topic 8 was included in the Funding Opportunity Announcement, but no proposals were funded in this area because the topic was initiated by the Army Research Office (ARO), and ARO dropped out of the program.

Defense (OSD) priorities are also reflected. Box 1-2 shows the topics announced for the 2018 funding cycle, and Appendix B lists all topics funded over the years. On the 2018 list, "Economic Interdependence and Security" and "Alliances and Burden-Sharing" are examples of topic areas that reflect OSD priorities, based on the National Defense Strategy. Since 2017, service branch program managers also have been taking a more active role in the white paper review process, including nominating reviewers and providing recommendations on the ranking of projects to fund. For further discussion of the processes involved in awarding and managing the Minerva grants, see Chapter 3.

Figure 1-3 shows the number of Minerva projects funded by DoD, by year. As the result of funding delays due to a variety of causes, such as the government appropriations process and the involvement of several entities in the execution of grants, the committee found that attributing a start year to a grant was not always straightforward. In 2011, for example, DoD's funding was delayed, but some "2010 funds" were still available for use. While no awards were made in 2011, some grants started in that year.

In 2014, DoD launched a pilot program that involved diverting some of the Minerva funds to support research at Professional Military Education Institutions, such as West Point and the Air Force Academy. Those grants have since been discontinued. In 2017, a new collaboration with the U.S.

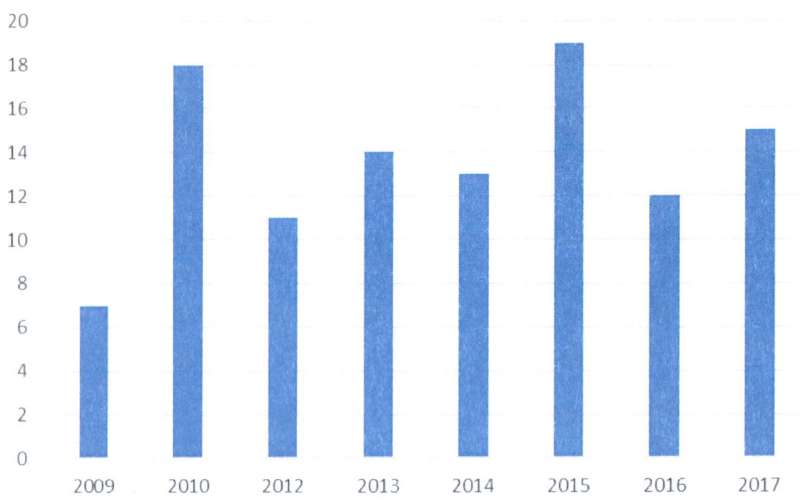

FIGURE 1-3 Number of Minerva projects funded, by year.

Institute of Peace was launched that provided dissertation fellowships and early-career scholar awards for research related to peace, conflict, security, and stability. These awards were not included in the committee's evaluation.

As noted earlier, initially, the projects funded by the Minerva program were fairly large (several million dollars), and they lasted an average of 5 years. Over the years, emphasis shifted from large consortia to smaller projects, with an average budget of around $1.5 million and lasting 3 to 4 years. Figure 1-4 shows this shift in the average grant sizes.

Table 1-2 provides a more detailed look at the Minerva grant solicitations, by the year in which they were issued. Note that in some cases, the awards were announced the following calendar year. Because of logistical and contracting constraints, the solicitations have been issued by different DoD branches over time.

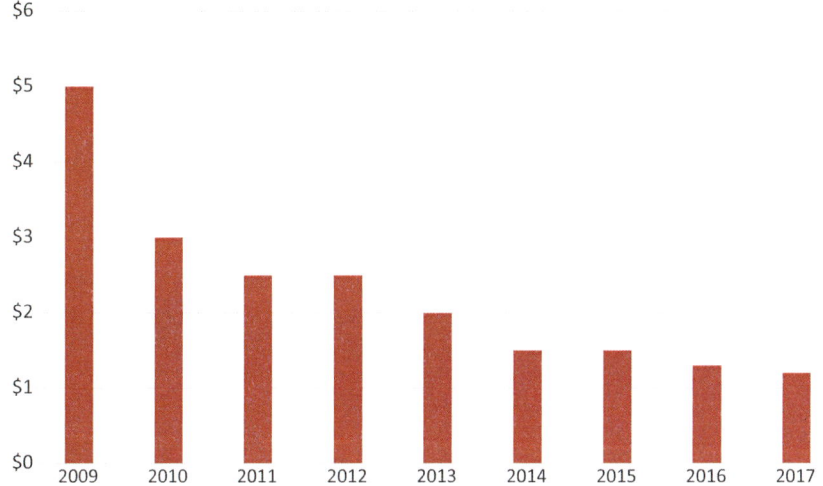

FIGURE 1-4 Average size of Minerva grants, by year, in millions of dollars.
NOTE: One very large grant of around $20 million was awarded in 2008. To allow for a clearer representation of the differences across the years 2009 to 2017, that project is not included in this figure.
SOURCE: Nair (2018).

TABLE 1-2 Overview of the Characteristics of Minerva Grant Solicitations, by Year

Year/Solicitation Title	Issuing Agency	Total Amount of Funding Specified in Grant Announcement	Size of Awards Specified in Grant Announcement
2008 Broad Agency Announcement (W911NF-08-R-0007)	DoD Army Research Office	$50,000,000 over 5 years	Awards of $500,000 to $3,000,000 per year, with typical awards in the range of $1,000,000 to $1,500,000 per year
2008 Solicitation for Social and Behavioral Dimensions of National Security, Conflict, and Cooperation (NSCC) (NSF 08-594)	National Science Foundation	$8,000,000	1 to 5 workshops ($50,000 to $150,000); 8 to 10 small awards (total of $500,000 over 2 to 3 years); 1 to 3 large awards ($2,000,000 per year)
2011 Broad Agency Announcement (W911NF-11-R-0011)	DoD Army Research Office	$35,000,000 over 5 years	Single-investigator small-team awards from $30,000 to $500,000 per year, with typical awards in the range of $100,000 to $300,000 per year; large-team awards from $500,000 to $2,000,000 per year, with typical awards in the range of $1,000,000 to $1,500,000 per year
2012 Broad Agency Announcement (ONR BAA 12-016)	DoD Office of Naval Research	$24,000,000 over 3 years	15 awards of $300,000 to $1,500,000 per year for 3 to 5 years
2013 Broad Agency Announcement (ONR BAA 13-024)	DoD Office of Naval Research	$15,000,000 over 3 years	12 awards of $200,000 to $1,500,000 per year for 3 to 5 years
2014 Broad Agency Announcement (ONR BAA 14-013)	DoD Office of Naval Research	$8,000,0000 over 3 years	5 to 7 awards of $150,000 to $1,000,000 per year for 3 to 5 years
2016 Funding Opportunity Announcement (FOA #WHS-AD-FOA-16-01)	DoD Washington Headquarters Services/Acquisition Directorate	$15,000,000 over 3 years	10 to 12 awards of $150,000 to $1,000,000 per year for 3 to 5 years

2017 Funding Opportunity Announcement (FOA #WHS-AD-FOA-17-01)	DoD Washington Headquarters Services/Acquisition Directorate	$15,000,000 over 3 years	10 to 12 awards of $150,000 to $1,000,000 per year for 3 to 5 years
2018 Funding Opportunity Announcement (FOA #WHS-AD-FOA-18)	DoD Washington Headquarters Services/Acquisition Directorate	$15,000,000 over 3 years	10 to 12 awards of $150,000 to $1,000,000 per year for 3 to 5 years

NOTE: The table summarizes award information from the grant announcements. The characteristics of the grants awarded do not necessarily reflect these parameters.

CHARGE TO THE COMMITTEE

As the Minerva Research Initiative completes its first decade, DoD considers it important to look back and evaluate the program's successes and challenges over the years. DoD would also like to determine the best path for the program going forward, consistent with its original vision, as well as the needs for basic research in the service branches and the policy focus of OSD. To that end, the National Academies of Sciences, Engineering, and Medicine was asked to convene a committee to (1) assess the program's impact on the scientific community and on DoD stakeholders, (2) identify emerging opportunities to improve the efficiency of the program's administration, and (3) provide guidance on strategies for addressing the diverse needs of different constituencies so as to maximize the contribution of social science research to addressing the security challenges faced by DoD. The committee's full statement of task is shown in Box 1-3.

The committee included experts in program review and evaluation and social scientists with broad, interdisciplinary backgrounds and experience with grants and journal publication standards in a range of disciplines. Several of the committee members also had in-depth experience with federal science-funding mechanisms.

BOX 1-3
Statement of Task

The National Academies of Sciences, Engineering and Medicine will conduct a program evaluation of the Minerva Research Initiative (MRI) that resides within the Office of the Secretary of Defense. The committee will be tasked to address: (1) quality and impact of the program, (2) processes and procedures that may affect the success of the program, and (3) direction and vision based on the challenges of the world today. This will be an unclassified study.

Study Part I. – Quality and Impact
The first part of the program review will look at the historical context of the program, specifically at the quality of the research it has supported and the impact of funding such research, based on the outputs the program has facilitated. Questions relevant here include:

1. What has been accomplished after eight years of the program in terms of (a) basic science advances; (b) policy-relevant insights or tools for the security community?
2. What is the quality of research funded and its impact on the social science knowledge base, as well as on public understandings of the problems addressed by the researchers?

BOX 1-3 Continued

3. What challenges has MRI confronted in generating interest in participation in the program among basic social scientists and how has it addressed those challenges?
4. Has MRI effectively fostered the development of communities working on social science issues around security, and the creation of organizational structures and processes to advance this research?
5. What communities have benefited from MRI-supported research and how would those benefits be characterized?
6. Is MRI unique as a funding source or are there other agencies/organizations funding similar research at similar levels?
7. What is the relationship between basic research and applied insights of the research that MRI seeks to generate?

Study Part II. – Program and Function
The second part of the study will look at program-related process issues that impact the success of the program and will consider questions such as:

1. How does the proposal review process compare to similar programs at NSF, DHS, and processes that the service branch research agencies use?
2. How does the project implementation and management process compare to similar programs at NSF, DHS, and the service branch research agencies?
3. Are the right projects being prioritized for (a) national security needs, generally speaking; and (b) the particular missions of the service branch research agencies?
4. Is the program successful in connecting researchers to policymakers?
5. How might the program improve outreach and integration of basic research insights into DoD?

Study Part III. – Direction and Vision
The third part of the study will look at how the initial charge of the program reflects the challenges of our world today, looking specifically at how Parts I and II of the study can best address the contemporary issues faced by DoD.

1. Has the vision that initiated MRI evolved, or are there ways in which it needs to evolve to better address contemporary security concerns?
2. How can MRI shape the future of basic research in social science around the issues of security?
3. How is MRI influencing academic disciplines in their engagement with security and facilitating interdisciplinary and cross-disciplinary research and are their opportunities for improving in these efforts?
4. How might MRI cultivate the interests of young scholars in working with DoD on social science security issues?

To guide its work and help organize its thinking, the committee developed a set of research questions based on its statement of task:

- How well does Minerva operate, and how does it compare with other basic social science research programs?
- What research output has been supported by Minerva grants, and what is the quality of Minerva-supported research?
- Should and how can DoD make better use of the insights and tools/products of Minerva-supported research?
- Should and how can DoD change (1) the vision of Minerva; (2) the process for setting priorities/selecting research topics; and (3) the selection of projects to fund so as to meet contemporary, changing national security challenges, as well as the needs of each service branch, more effectively?
- Should and how can DoD increase—deepen and broaden—the engagement of social scientists in research relevant to national security?

To address its charge, the committee undertook a range of information-gathering activities, discussed in Chapter 2. Chapter 3 focuses on the processes involved in the Minerva program, including how it operates and how it compares with other similar programs that fund basic social science research. Chapter 4 provides an overview of the research supported by the program, including the quantity and quality of the outputs generated. Finally, Chapter 5 focuses on future directions for the program, including ways of broadening the use of the research and reliance on the expertise of the Minerva grantees, increasing the engagement of social scientists with the program, and any changes needed to the program's vision and goals going forward. The committee's recommendations are presented in Chapters 3 and 5.

Table 1-3 shows how the research questions listed above map to the committee's statement of task and how the report is organized to address these questions.

TABLE 1-3 Minerva Program Evaluation Questions from the Statement of Task and Key Research Questions

	Research Questions Developed by the Committee				
Question from the Statement of Task	How well does Minerva operate, and how does it compare with other basic social science research programs?	What research output has been supported by Minerva grants, and what is the quality of Minerva-supported research?	Should and how can DoD make better use of the insights and tools/products of Minerva-supported research?	Should and how can DoD change (1) the vision of Minerva; (2) the process for setting priorities/selecting research topics; and (3) the selection of projects to fund so as to meet contemporary, changing national security challenges, as well as the needs of each service branch, more effectively?	Should and how can DoD increase—deepen and broaden—the engagement of social scientists in research relevant to national security?
	Chapter 3	Chapter 4	Chapter 5	Chapters 3 and 5	Chapter 5
Part I. Quality and Impact					
1. What has been accomplished after eight years of the program in terms of (a) basic science advances; (b) policy-relevant insights or tools for the security community?		X	X		
2. What is the quality of research funded and its impact on the social science knowledge base, as well as on public understandings of the problems addressed by the researchers?		X			

continued

TABLE 1-3 Continued

Question from the Statement of Task	Research Questions Developed by the Committee				
	How well does Minerva operate, and how does it compare with other basic social science research programs?	What research output has been supported by Minerva grants, and what is the quality of Minerva-supported research?	Should and how can DoD make better use of the insights and tools/products of Minerva-supported research?	Should and how can DoD change (1) the vision of Minerva; (2) the process for setting priorities/selecting research topics; and (3) the selection of projects to fund so as to meet contemporary, changing national security challenges, as well as the needs of each service branch, more effectively?	Should and how can DoD increase—deepen and broaden—the engagement of social scientists in research relevant to national security?
	Chapter 3	Chapter 4	Chapter 5	Chapters 3 and 5	Chapter 5
3. What challenges has Minerva confronted in generating interest in participation in the program among basic social scientists and how has it addressed those challenges?				X	X
4. Has Minerva effectively fostered the development of communities working on social science issues around security, and the creation of organizational structures and processes to advance this research?		X			X
5. What communities have benefited from Minerva-supported research and how would those benefits be characterized?		X	X		

6. Is Minerva unique as a funding source or are there other agencies/organizations funding similar research at similar levels?	X		
7. What is the relationship between basic research and applied insights of the research that Minerva seeks to generate?		X	X

Part II. Program and Function

1. How does the proposal review process compare to similar programs at NSF, DHS, and processes that the service branch research agencies use?	X		
2. How does the project implementation and management process compare to similar programs at NSF, DHS, and the service branch research agencies?	X		
3. Are the right projects being prioritized for (a) national security needs, generally speaking; and (b) the particular missions of the service branch research agencies?		X	X
4. Is the program successful in connecting researchers to policymakers?		X	X
5. How might the program improve outreach and integration of basic research insights into DoD?		X	

continued

23

TABLE 1-3 Continued

Question from the Statement of Task	How well does Minerva operate, and how does it compare with other basic social science research programs?	What research output has been supported by Minerva grants, and what is the quality of Minerva-supported research?	Should and how can DoD make better use of the insights and tools/products of Minerva-supported research?	Should and how can DoD change (1) the vision of Minerva; (2) the process for setting priorities/selecting research topics; and (3) the selection of projects to fund so as to meet contemporary, changing national security challenges, as well as the needs of each service branch, more effectively?	Should and how can DoD increase—deepen and broaden—the engagement of social scientists in research relevant to national security?
	Chapter 3	Chapter 4	Chapter 5	Chapters 3 and 5	Chapter 5
Part III. Direction and Vision					
1. Has the vision that initiated MRI evolved, or are there ways in which it needs to evolve to better address contemporary security concerns?				X	
2. How can Minerva shape the future of basic research in social science around the issues of security?			X	X	X
3. How is Minerva influencing academic disciplines in their engagement with security and facilitating interdisciplinary and cross-disciplinary research and are their opportunities for improving in these efforts?					X

4. How might Minerva cultivate the interests of young scholars in working with DoD on social science security issues?   X

2

Overview of the Committee's Information-Gathering Activities

As noted in Chapter 1, the committee undertook several information-gathering activities to gain an in-depth understanding of the Minerva Research Initiative and perceptions of the program. This chapter describes those activities, which included (1) reviews of Department of Defense (DoD) and other public records; (2) interviews with current and former DoD staff; (3) a grantee survey; (4) a survey of administrators of sponsored research at academic institutions; (5) the annual Minerva Conference; and (6) public information-gathering sessions held at the National Academies of Sciences, Engineering, and Medicine. Along with the data sources described in this chapter, the committee also issued a public call for comments, which was posted on the National Academies website and circulated in electronic newsletters. In this chapter, descriptions of the above information-gathering activities are followed by a discussion of the limitations of the committee's evaluation.

Table 2-1 provides an overview of how the committee's key research questions, discussed in Chapter 1, align with the main data sources that yielded information with which to address these questions. Table 2-2 shows the detailed list of questions included in the committee's statement of task and the data sources used to address them.

REVIEWS OF DEPARTMENT OF DEFENSE AND OTHER PUBLIC RECORDS

The committee asked DoD to provide any available historical documentation about the program, including information about the grants that have been awarded over the years. The documents received from DoD, including

TABLE 2-1 Key Research Questions for the Minerva Program Evaluation and Relevant Data Sources

Research Question	DoD and Other Public Records	Interviews with DoD Staff	Grantee Survey and Grantee Conference	Survey of Sponsored Research Administrators	Input from National Security Experts and Other Stakeholders	Discussions with Other Funders
1. How well does Minerva operate, and how does it compare with other basic social science research programs?	X	X	X	X	X	X
2. What research output has been supported by Minerva grants, and what is the quality of Minerva-supported research?	X	X	X	X	X	
3. Should and how can DoD make better use of the insights and tools/products of Minerva-supported research?	X	X	X	X	X	
4. Should and how can DoD change (1) the vision of Minerva; (2) the process for setting priorities/selecting research topics; and (3) the selection of projects to fund so as to meet contemporary, changing national security challenges, as well as the needs of each service branch, more effectively?	X	X		X	X	
5. Should and how can DoD increase—deepen and broaden—the engagement of social scientists in research relevant to national security?	X	X	X	X	X	X

TABLE 2-2 Minerva Program Evaluation Detailed Questions from the Statement of Task and Relevant Data Sources

Question from the Statement of Task	DoD and Other Public Records	Interviews with DoD Staff	Grantee Survey and Grantee Conference	Survey of Sponsored Research Administrators	Input from National Security Experts and Other Stakeholders	Discussions with Other Funders
Part I. Quality and Impact						
1. What has been accomplished after eight years of the program in terms of (a) basic science advances; (b) policy-relevant insights or tools for the security community?	X	X	X		X	
2. What is the quality of research funded and its impact on the social science knowledge base, as well as on public understandings of the problems addressed by the researchers?	X	X	X		X	
3. What challenges has Minerva confronted in generating interest in participation in the program among basic social scientists and how has it addressed those challenges?		X	X	X		
4. Has Minerva effectively fostered the development of communities working on social science issues around security, and the creation of organizational structures and processes to advance this research?	X	X	X	X	X	
5. What communities have benefited from Minerva-supported research and how would those benefits be characterized?	X	X	X	X	X	

continued

29

TABLE 2-2 Continued

	Data Source				
Question from the Statement of Task	DoD and Other Public Records	Interviews with DoD Staff	Grantee Survey and Grantee Conference	Survey of Sponsored Research Administrators	Input from National Security Experts and Other Stakeholders	Discussions with Other Funders
6. Is Minerva unique as a funding source or are there other agencies/organizations funding similar research at similar levels?	X	X	X	X		X
7. What is the relationship between basic research and applied insights of the research that Minerva seeks to generate?	X	X	X		X	
Part II. Program and Function						
1. How does the proposal review process compare to similar programs at NSF, DHS, and processes that the service branch research agencies use?	X	X	X	X		X
2. How does the project implementation and management process compare to similar programs at NSF, DHS, and the service branch research agencies?	X	X	X	X		X
3. Are the right projects being prioritized for (a) national security needs, generally speaking; and (b) the particular missions of the service branch research agencies?	X	X			X	
4. Is the program successful in connecting researchers to policymakers?	X	X	X			
5. How might the program improve outreach and integration of basic research insights into DoD?	X	X	X		X	

Part III. Direction and Vision				
1. Has the vision that initiated MRI evolved, or are there ways in which it needs to evolve to better address contemporary security concerns?	X	X		X
2. How can Minerva shape the future of basic research in social science around the issues of security?		X	X	X
3. How is Minerva influencing academic disciplines in their engagement with security and facilitating interdisciplinary and cross-disciplinary research and are their opportunities for improving in these efforts?	X	X	X	
4. How might Minerva cultivate the interests of young scholars in working with DoD on social science security issues?		X	X	X

memorandums, speeches, and presentations, provided valuable background and contextual information about the program. To complement this information, National Academies staff compiled additional background information and available records relevant to the Minerva program from public sources.

The committee was unable to obtain a definitive list of all the Minerva grants from DoD because no centralized database of the funded studies exists. The primary reason for the lack of such a database is that, as described in Chapter 1, the Minerva program is a collaboration among several units within DoD, and individual grants are executed and overseen by program managers based at the basic research organizations of the three military service branches: the Air Force Office of Scientific Research (AFOSR), the Army Research Office (ARO), and the Office of Naval Research (ONR). As noted in Chapter 1 and discussed in detail in Chapter 3, the role of the service branches has changed over the years; however, the program managers have always followed their own branch's contracting, record keeping, and reporting practices. DoD began work on developing a central database of the Minerva grants around the time when the committee's evaluation began, but this work was still ongoing when the evaluation was completed.

To compensate for the lack of a database of grants, National Academies staff worked with the Minerva program director to compile a list of grantees and information about the characteristics of the grants based on public records and other DoD materials, such as the Minerva Research Summaries from Minerva Conferences. A list of grants thereby derived is included in Appendix C and was used for the committee's grantee survey (described below), as well as for other analyses included in this report. However, questions remained throughout the course of the study about whether this list of grantees was truly comprehensive.

The committee also attempted to obtain progress reports and final reports submitted to DoD by grantees as part of their reporting requirements. Again, these records are stored not in a central repository but at the service branches, in accordance with their differing practices. The committee was able to obtain an annual or final report for only about half of the grants, and these were primarily grants managed by ARO and ONR. While the reports obtained provided information useful to the committee, the missing reports and the inconsistent content in the reports that were available made them inadequate as a source for a systematic understanding of the quantity and quality of the outputs produced by the grants. For this reason, the committee requested a list of outputs from the grantees as part of the grantee survey discussed below.

INTERVIEWS WITH DEPARTMENT OF DEFENSE STAFF

To complement the information obtained from available records related to the Minerva program and learn about the perspectives of program staff, the committee conducted individual telephone interviews with current and former DoD staff involved with the Minerva Research Initiative over the years. Interviewees included current and former Minerva program directors, staff from the Basic Research Office and the Office of Policy, Minerva program managers within the military service branches, and others affiliated with the program.

A total of 14 telephone interviews were conducted between September 4 and October 8, 2018. Depending on the extent of current involvement in the program, interviews lasted from 40 minutes to 2 hours. The interviews were conducted by a National Academies senior program officer using a semi-structured interview guide developed by the committee. Appendix D shows the detailed interview guide; the broad topics covered in the interviews were

- structure and management of the program,
- successes and challenges of the program,
- quality of the research funded,
- use of the research funded,
- selection of topics to fund,
- selection of projects to fund,
- broadening of engagement among social scientists, and
- vision of Minerva.

In addition to answering the questions asked of all interviewees, Minerva program managers and the current Minerva program director were asked to describe in detail the steps involved in managing the program. They were asked to describe the processes involved in

- selecting topics to fund,
- soliciting submissions,
- reviewing proposal submissions,
- selecting projects to fund,
- awarding the grants,
- managing the grants and monitoring grant progress and performance,
- supporting dissemination activities, and
- supporting translation activities.

GRANTEE SURVEY

The grantee survey was a census of all Minerva grantees on the list of grantees compiled in collaboration with DoD, including projects administered through the National Science Foundation (NSF). The survey was conducted by the National Opinion Research Center (NORC) at the University of Chicago.

For each of the grants, the principal investigator (PI) of record was asked to respond to the survey. PIs who had been awarded more than one

Minerva grant over the years (six cases) received one invitation to complete the survey and were asked to think about all of their grants when answering the questions. The result was a universe of 102 PIs.

Appendix E includes the wording of each of the questions on the survey, which covered

- experiences with Minerva grants compared with other social science grant programs,
- broadening of engagement among social scientists,
- challenges associated with conducting research relevant to national security,
- opportunities resulting from the grant, and
- outputs resulting from the research.

The survey was conducted via web, and potential respondents were initially contacted by email. NORC sent all individuals identified as PIs an email inviting them to participate in the study and conducted successful locating searches to identify valid email addresses for those whose contact information (initially compiled by National Academies staff) was invalid. For nonresponders, up to four additional emails were sent urging them to complete the survey. The first round of nonresponder prompt emails was sent 2 days after the initial email. For the following 3 weeks, each subsequent nonresponder prompt email was sent 1 week after the previous one. Remaining nonrespondents who failed to complete the survey after the four additional email prompts received a hard-copy letter via FedEx encouraging their participation.

Initially identified PIs who felt that a colleague (such as a co-PI) was better equipped to complete the survey were offered the opportunity to delegate the task accordingly. In the initial recruitment and subsequent reminder emails, the originally identified PIs were informed that they could provide the study team with contact information for such a colleague. Those to whom the survey was delegated then received a tailored recruitment email explaining that a colleague had delegated the survey to them. Delegated grantees who failed to complete the survey received up to the maximum number of nonresponder emails in accordance with the study's nonrespondent prompting protocol.

In addition to responding to the survey questions, grantees were asked to provide a list of all of the publications and other outputs (such as manuscripts, presentations, briefings, and testimony) that had resulted from their Minerva grant. To make this task as easy as possible, respondents were offered several mechanisms for completing it. One option was to submit this information as part of the survey, by typing it or copying and pasting it into the web survey fields. The other options offered were to upload a curriculum vitae (CV) with the grant-related items highlighted or to email a list or a CV to a Minerva survey email inbox. The data collection contractor also accommodated additional requests, such as providing a link to a grant website. Given the higher burden associated with submitting this information (relative to answering the survey questions), grantees who provided responses to the survey questions but did not submit their lists of outputs received up to two additional email reminders to provide this further information. The information obtained about the grant outputs was then compiled from the different sources and organized into a database.

Table 2-3 shows the completion rates for the survey, along with the numbers of partials and nonresponse/refusals. Of the 102 grantees asked to complete the survey, 76 did so (a 75% completion rate). Three additional grantees submitted partially completed surveys, which were included in the analyses described in this report whenever possible.

Of those who completed the survey, 67 (88%) also responded to the request for information on grant outputs. This number includes 4 grantees who as yet had no outputs. For such a relatively complex and burdensome request on a web survey, some amount of misreporting is to be expected. It is possible that some PIs inadvertently reported outputs that were closely related to their Minerva research but, technically, were supported by another source of funding. It appears more likely, however, that Minerva-supported outputs were unintentionally omitted from the lists provided by PIs, and thus underreported. Comparison of the lists provided in response to the grantee survey with lists provided on progress and final reports to DoD appears to suggest that this may be the case. However, the previously discussed limitations of the information obtained from the latter reports prevent a more complete analysis of or correction for survey misreporting.

TABLE 2-3 Rates of Completion, Partial Completion, and Nonresponse/Refusal for the Grantee Survey

	Number of Grantees	Percent
Total	102	100
Completes	76	75
Grant Outputs Reported	67	88
Partial Completes	3	3
Nonresponse/Refusals	23	22

NOTES: The 67 grantees that reported grant outputs include 4 grants that had recently been awarded and as yet had no outputs. The percentage of grant outputs reported (n = 67) is shown as a percentage of the number of completes (n = 76).

The lack of a fully accurate and comprehensive list of all papers, presentations, and other materials and activities resulting from each Minerva grant due to both nonresponse and misreporting on the grantee survey limited the committee's ability to quantify the outputs of the grants. Further limiting what could be learned about the quantity of outputs was the fact that the program is relatively new and that many of the grants were still in progress at the time of this study (grants awarded from 2015 through 2017 represented approximately 40 percent of the projects funded). In addition, it is possible that grant-funded research tends to be more highly cited on average than research that is not grant-funded if grants make more resources available to projects, especially for dissemination. Thus, one limitation of the committee's analysis is that the outputs could not be rigorously compared with outputs from other research, and had to be discussed in the context of academic research productivity in general. Nonetheless, the committee was able to gain a solid understanding of the breadth and quality of the outputs (as discussed in Chapter 4) and to draw conclusions that should be relatively robust to the limitations of the available data.

Table 2-4 shows the rates of response to the survey questions and to the request for information on grant outputs by several key grantee characteristics. Response rates overall were high, but there were some differences by subgroup. The rates were highest among the grantees who received funding during the first few years of the program (2009–2012) and lowest among those who received funding during later years but prior to 2017 (2013–2016). Response rates were particularly high among the early NSF grantees and low among grantees whose projects were overseen by AFOSR.

To enable comparison of response rates by the PI's academic discipline, the field of doctoral degree was used as a proxy. Some fields that were represented by only one or two grantees were grouped together to maintain confidentiality. "Other social science fields" includes such fields as anthropology, demography, criminology, and geography, while "other fields" includes earth and ocean sciences, engineering, law, and physics. Response rates were lowest among those with degrees in mathematics and computer sciences.

To compare response rates by the seniority of the PIs, the Scopus database was consulted to determine the year of the PI's first peer-reviewed publication, which was used as a rough measure of seniority (for discussion of the limitations of the Scopus database, see Chapter 4). Response rates were highest among PIs whose first peer-reviewed publication appeared between 1995 and 2008, in other words, among midcareer researchers. The number of publications in Scopus was used as a proxy for researcher productivity, and the number of citations in Scopus was used as a proxy

TABLE 2-4 Rates of Response to the Grantee Survey, by Grantee Characteristics

	Completed Survey Questions (%)	Provided Information on Outputs (%)	Number of Grantees
Grant Start Year			
2009–2012	84	65	37
2013–2016	73	65	52
2017	77	69	13
Program Manager			
Air Force Office of Scientific Research	50	39	18
Army Research Office	79	64	33
Office of Naval Research	85	76	33
National Science Foundation	89	78	18
Principal Investigator's Academic Discipline			
Economics	75	63	8
Mathematics and Computer Sciences	58	58	12
Political Science	81	77	53
Psychology	73	36	11
Sociology	83	83	6
Other Social Science Fields	83	50	6
Other Fields	83	33	6
Principal Investigator's Earliest Peer-Reviewed Publication (Seniority)			
1968–1994	72	58	36
1995–2008	81	72	54
2009–present	75	58	12
Number of Publications in Scopus			
1–17	82	68	34
18–40	79	73	33
41–421	71	57	35
Number of Citations in Scopus			
1–295	82	67	33
296–1,219	79	76	33
1,220–15,825	70	52	33

for influence. Rates of response to both the survey and the request for information on outputs were lowest among researchers with the most publications and highest number of citations.

Open-ended responses were coded with a coding scheme developed by NORC and approved by the committee. Responses were double-coded and then reviewed to ensure intercoder reliability. When coders disagreed about a code, the project team met to discuss and reconcile the code.

The survey was designed to allow respondents to skip any questions they did not wish to answer, including those set up in a Yes/No format. As is typical for surveys with similar setups that imply a "check all that apply" request, for some questions a subset of respondents selected Yes for a few items and then moved on to the next screen without selecting a response for the rest of the items. Based on the context and intent of these questions, prior experience with similar missing data, and prior experience with similar questions, the data collection contractor recommended recoding missing responses as No in cases in which the respondent selected at least one Yes response to questions of this type.

NORC provided a fully labeled datafile of the survey data for the committee. Frequency distributions are shown in Appendix E.

SURVEY OF ADMINISTRATORS OF SPONSORED RESEARCH AT ACADEMIC INSTITUTIONS

The survey of administrators of sponsored research was a census of 222 administrators at institutions with "highest research activity" and "higher research activity" based on the Carnegie Classification of Institutions of Higher Education, a framework for categorizing academic institutions in the United States (Indiana University Center for Postsecondary Research, 2016). The person asked to complete the survey was the director of the office of sponsored programs (or equivalent) at universities where a position of this type existed. In cases in which this position did not exist, the vice president for research or dean of research was contacted. In some cases, it was necessary to make a judgment call about the most appropriate person to contact, but as with the grantee survey, sample members were given the opportunity to delegate the survey to someone else if one of their colleagues was better suited to respond.

Appendix F includes the wording of each of the survey questions, which addressed

- experiences with Minerva grants compared with other social science grant programs,
- broadening of engagement among social scientists, and
- perceptions of research relevant to national security.

NORC carried out the data collection for this survey using a list of universities and target individuals identified by the committee. The data collection and processing procedures for this survey were similar to the approach used for the grantee survey. The only notable difference was that instead of a FedEx reminder, an additional email prompt was sent to nonresponders to this survey. Table 2-5 shows the completion rates for the survey. Out of 222 administrators, 88 completed the survey (a 40% completion rate). An additional 18 individuals submitted partially completed surveys, which were included in the committee's analyses. Table 2-6 shows that the response rates by institution type (highest versus higher research activity) were similar.

Missing data for items in questions with a Yes/No format were handled as with the grantee survey. NORC provided a fully labeled datafile of the survey data for the committee. Frequency distributions, along with the wording of the questions, are shown in Appendix F.

TABLE 2-5 Rates of Completion, Partial Completion, and Nonresponse/Refusal for the Survey of Administrators of Sponsored Research

	Number of Administrators	Percent
Total	222	100
Completes	88	40
Partial Completes	18	8
Nonresponse/Refusals	116	52

TABLE 2-6 Rates of Response to the Survey of Administrators of Sponsored Research, by Institution Type

Institution Type	Number of Administrators	Completed or Partially Completed Survey (%)
Highest research activity	115	46
Higher research activity	107	50
Overall	222	48

MINERVA CONFERENCE

On September 26–27, 2018, three committee members and a National Academies staff member attended the annual conference of Minerva grantees, held in Washington, DC. The conference featured presentations from a subset of the grantees and breakout sessions to discuss the National Defense Strategy. Time also was set aside for the committee to describe its evaluation and solicit input in the form of a floor discussion. Participation in this event provided a valuable opportunity for the committee to gain an in-depth understanding of the grantees' work, listen to their questions and comments, and experience firsthand the Minerva program's main dissemination event.

PUBLIC INFORMATION-GATHERING SESSIONS

Input obtained from stakeholders and experts during public meetings with the committee was an important source of information for the committee's evaluation. Efforts were made to reach out to a broad range of stakeholders with diverse viewpoints. The committee met with grantees, national security experts, representatives of social science organizations, staff from other government agencies and organizations with similar social science grant programs, and others. These stakeholders provided valuable background information and perspectives that informed the committee's deliberations. Appendix G lists the individuals who provided input during these public meetings, held on January 16, April 12, July 19, and October 2, 2018.

LIMITATIONS OF THE COMMITTEE'S EVALUATION

In addition to the data availability and quality challenges described above, several overall limitations are associated with the committee's evaluation.

First, as is always the case with a study of this type that does not involve a randomized or quasi-experimental design, it was not possible to draw causal inferences about the impact or effectiveness of the Minerva program. The committee considered constructing a comparison group of academic researchers in social science fields, but ultimately determined that it was not feasible to do so in a rigorous way that would hold up to scrutiny. Thus there was no valid basis for ascertaining the counterfactual—the research that would have been conducted (and by whom) in the absence of the Minerva program.

Second, while 10 years into the program's operation might appear to be a timely point for an evaluation, significant changes to the program's structure and functioning were introduced in the same year that this study was launched (see Chapters 1 and 3). Thus it was difficult to obtain a good understanding of the processes involved in the program, and particularly to disentangle perceptions about aspects of the program that predated the changes from the program's current characteristics. More important, because the changes were so recent, it was not possible to assess how well the new approach was functioning.

Third, because of DoD's confidentiality policies, the evaluation did not include a survey of those who had applied for Minerva funding but did not receive grants. Nor did the evaluation include a survey of social science researchers who conduct research relevant to national security but have never applied for a Minerva grant.

Acknowledging these limitations, the committee did reach out to a broad range of stakeholders and issued a call for comments during the course of the study. Through the mechanisms described in this chapter, the committee was able to amass a substantial volume of information and input reflecting diverse perspectives. As with any National Academies study, the findings and recommendations in this report are based on the collective judgment and expertise of the committee, as informed by the available information.

3

Processes of the Minerva Program

This chapter provides an overview of the processes involved in the awarding and management of the Minerva Research Initiative grants, including (1) selecting topics for research funding, (2) soliciting submissions, (3) reviewing proposal submissions (white papers and full proposals), (4) selecting awardees, (5) awarding the grants, (6) managing the grants and monitoring grant progress and performance, (7) supporting dissemination activities, and (8) supporting translation activities. This overview is followed by the committee's evaluation of ways in which these processes could be refined to enhance the performance and efficiency of the program going forward.

As discussed in Chapter 1, the Minerva Research Initiative was envisioned as a unique collaboration between research and policy divisions within the Department of Defense (DoD). The vision for the program was to work together to support basic research on social science issues deemed to be important to national security, and then find ways of integrating insights from this research into the policy-making context. The collaboration was structured to involve the research units and program managers from three military service branches: the Air Force Office of Scientific Research (AFOSR), the Army Research Office (ARO), and the Office of Naval Research (ONR). The grants are executed through the service branches, with the program managers providing technical oversight for the projects. Figure 3-1 illustrates the organizational structure of the Minerva program. At the time this study was initiated, the ARO program manager served as interim director for Minerva. When a new deputy director was brought in, the interim director became assistant director, but the assistant director position was dropped when ARO

```
┌─────────────────────────────────┐              ┌─────────────────────────────────┐
│ Assistant Secretary of Defense  │              │ Director of Defense Research and│
│  for Strategy, Plans and        │              │ Engineering for Research &      │
│  Capabilities                   │              │ Technology                      │
└─────────────────────────────────┘              └─────────────────────────────────┘
              ↕                                                  ↕
┌─────────────────────────────────┐              ┌─────────────────────────────────┐
│ Deputy Assistant Secretary of   │              │ Deputy Director for Research,   │
│ Defense for Strategy and Force  │              │ Technology and Laboratories     │
│ Development                     │              │                                 │
└─────────────────────────────────┘              └─────────────────────────────────┘
              ↕                                                  ↕
┌─────────────────────────────────┐              ┌─────────────────────────────────┐
│            Strategy             │              │      Basic Research Office      │
└─────────────────────────────────┘              └─────────────────────────────────┘
                    ↘                                   ↙
                    ┌─────────────────────────────────┐
                    │ Minerva Research Initiative     │
                    │ Deputy Director                 │
                    └─────────────────────────────────┘
              ↙                       ↕                        ↘
┌──────────────────┐      ┌──────────────────┐       ┌──────────────────┐
│ Office of Naval  │      │ Air Force Office │       │ Army Research    │
│ Research         │      │ of Scientific    │       │ Office           │
│ Minerva Program  │      │ Research         │       │ Minerva Program  │
│ Manager          │      │ Minerva Program  │       │ Manager          │
│                  │      │ Manager          │       │                  │
└──────────────────┘      └──────────────────┘       └──────────────────┘
```

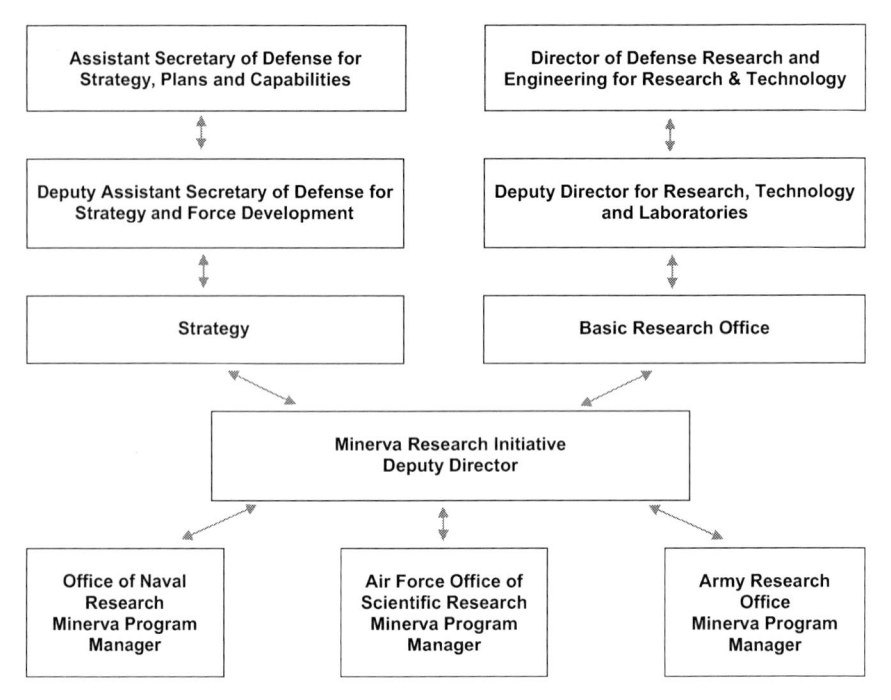

FIGURE 3-1 Organizational structure of the Minerva Research Initiative as of 2018. NOTES: The bottom row of the figure represents the military service branches. The Army withdrew its support as of October 1, 2018, and will no longer manage new grants. The Assistant Secretary of Defense for Strategy, Plans and Capabilities is in the Office of the Under Secretary of Defense for Policy (OUSD-Policy). The Director of Defense Research and Engineering for Research and Technology is in the Office of the Under Secretary for Research and Engineering (OUSD-R&E). Both OUSD-Policy and OUSD-R&E are units within the Office of the Secretary of Defense (OSD). The Minerva Research Initiative is housed in OSD and managed jointly by OUSD-Policy and OUSD-R&E.

pulled out of the program. Minerva is currently overseen by a "deputy" director instead of a director for administrative reasons, and aside from the deputy director, the Minerva program office contains no additional staff.

OVERVIEW OF PROGRAM PROCESSES

Until 2017, the Minerva program was overseen primarily by the Office of the Under Secretary of Defense for Policy (OUSD-Policy) and the Office of the Assistant Secretary of Defense for Research and Engineering (ASD-R&E) within the Office of the Secretary of Defense (OSD). The service branches were responsible primarily for executing and managing the

PROCESSES OF THE MINERVA PROGRAM 45

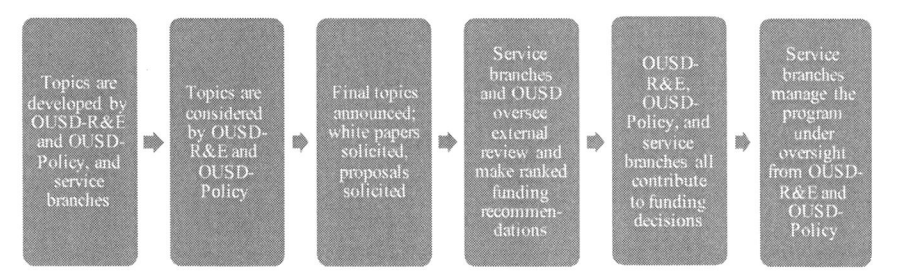

| Topics are developed by OUSD-R&E and OUSD-Policy, and service branches | → | Topics are considered by OUSD-R&E and OUSD-Policy | → | Final topics announced; white papers solicited, proposals solicited | → | Service branches and OUSD oversee external review and make ranked funding recommendations | → | OUSD-R&E, OUSD-Policy, and service branches all contribute to funding decisions | → | Service branches manage the program under oversight from OUSD-R&E and OUSD-Policy |

FIGURE 3-2 Sequence of steps currently involved in the Minerva program.
SOURCE: Adapted from Montgomery (2019).

grants and had a relatively minor influence on the white paper and proposal review processes. Beginning in 2017, DoD restructured the program to emphasize a more equal partnership between OSD and the service branches. The service branches are now involved in all aspects of grant operations. Table 1-1 in Chapter 1 shows the division of responsibilities before and after the restructuring.

Figure 3-2 shows the current sequence of steps involved in managing the program. The processes entailed in program operations, including the changes that have taken place over the years, are described in further detail below. This description of the program's processes was compiled on the basis of information provided by DoD staff involved with the program, including current and past Minerva directors and service branch program managers. Given that ARO was part of the Minerva Research Initiative from the beginning and was still part of the program when this evaluation was launched, the discussion of processes includes ARO's experiences.

Topic Selection

To ensure that the Minerva grants address knowledge gaps and national security needs, funding announcements highlight topics that represent questions of interest to DoD. Box 1-2 in Chapter 1 shows the topics included in the 2018 Funding Opportunity Announcement (FOA), while Appendix B shows all topics since 2008. The topics are broad, and proposals are not limited to the topics specified. The general themes are also relatively consistent from year to year. For example, the 2018 list of topics included "Sociopolitical (In)Stability, Resilience, and Recovery," while the 2017 list included "Societal Resilience & Sociopolitical (In)stability." Since 2018, the FOA has also discussed topic alignment with the National Defense Strategy.

As discussed, the process used for topic selection has changed over time from one that was top-down (from OSD to the military service branches) to one that is now more collaborative. Currently, the service branch program managers generate topics and then work with OSD to refine those topics and ensure that they also represent DoD-wide priorities.

The process for generating topics of interest varies by service branch and is dependent largely on the program managers' preferences. Suggestions for potential topics are gathered by email or discussion with other personnel and leadership in the service branches. Some service branch program managers focus on honing a particular topic over several years and finding what best accords with the service branch's and OSD's strategic vision. Other service branch program managers focus on balancing the priorities of their service branch and the objectives of the Minerva program while at the same time aligning potential topics with the portfolio of their own larger research program area.

The topics that originate in the service branches are nominated for inclusion in the FOA. The central Minerva program office may also solicit topics from within OSD. The Minerva program office reviews the draft topics and discusses them with the service branches and then with OSD before the list of topics is finalized.

Soliciting Submissions

Grant announcements are disseminated through grants.gov, which is a primary vehicle for distributing information about government grant research funding and is used by universities to learn about funding opportunities. In addition, information about the announcements is posted on the Minerva website, and the Minerva program office maintains a mailing list of individuals who have expressed an interest in receiving updates about the program. Typically, new Minerva funding opportunities are announced at the beginning of the calendar year; in 2018, however, the announcement was delayed until May because until then, the Minerva program office had only a part-time interim director in place.

Reviewing Proposal Submissions

As noted in Chapter 1, the Minerva program's proposal process consists of two stages. In the first stage, researchers are asked—but not required—to submit white papers briefly summarizing their proposals. Researchers whose white papers are deemed most competitive then receive an invitation to submit a full proposal.

The turnaround time for white paper submissions tends to be short, and full proposals are due a few months later. In 2018, because the FOA was not posted until May, the turnaround time for full proposals had to be condensed. Thus the FOA was posted on May 24, white papers were due on June 19, and full proposals were due on August 14. By contrast, in 2016 (a more typical year), the FOA was posted on January 12, white papers were due on February 29, and full proposals were due on July 1.

The 2018 criteria for reviewing proposals were

- scientific merit;
- relevance and potential contributions of the proposed research to areas of interest to DoD;
- potential impact, including potential for building new communities, new frameworks, and opportunities for dialogue;
- qualifications of principal investigators (PIs); and
- cost and value.

The 2018 FOA highlighted scientific merit and relevance as the two, equally important, principal criteria for evaluating proposals. Potential impact, PI qualifications, and cost and value were described as less important.

Prior to 2017, OSD took the lead in reviewing white papers. Under the changes instituted in 2017, the service branch program managers (in topic areas assigned to their branches) or the Minerva program office (in topic areas assigned to OSD) reviews white papers and decides who will be invited to submit full proposals. The white paper review involves the "responsible research area point of contact" (typically the service branch program manager) and one or more subject matter experts. DoD systems engineering and technical assistance contractors also may assist the responsible research area points of contact. The white papers that best meet the evaluation criteria are recommended to the OSD Minerva Steering Committee, which includes representatives from OSD and representatives from the service branches (Department of Defense Washington Headquarters Services/Acquisition Directorate, 2018, pp. 22–23). As noted, a subset of the researchers who submitted white papers are then invited to submit full proposals. For the 2018 funding cycle, DoD received 192 white papers and 52 full proposals.

The service branches now also have a larger role in reviewing full proposals, in collaboration with the Minerva director. In 2018, another OSD staff member, with a Ph.D. in political science, was invited to comment on the scientific merit of the proposals. The proposals are evaluated for policy relevance only after having been evaluated for scientific merit. Policy relevance may be used to decide between two proposals of equal scientific merit.

Within the service branches, each program manager recruits four to five people for the review panel that evaluates the proposals. Typically, the panel includes some outside academics, individuals with expertise in the topic area, and at least one DoD staff member. Depending on the topic areas and service branch requirements, some panels comprise larger or smaller numbers of academics or policy experts, some panels include academics from military colleges or universities, and some draw experts from within the relevant service branch (in addition to the service branch program manager leading the evaluation). Proposals are rated by the reviewers on a qualitative scale ranging from unacceptable to outstanding, based on the criteria described above.

The evaluation criteria and processes used by DoD from 2008 to 2018 appear to have remained fairly consistent, except for the structural changes introduced in 2017 and other minor changes over time. Details about the processes, however, do not exist in written form, except to the extent that they are captured in the FOAs.

Because some of the Minerva grants were managed by the National Science Foundation (NSF) when the program was first launched, and because NSF grants are familiar to many academic researchers conducting social science research, the processes used by NSF are also briefly described throughout this section. The survey results discussed later in this chapter provide some insight into how satisfaction with these processes compares between Minerva and NSF grantees. The surveys also asked about experiences with Department of Homeland Security (DHS) grants and other social science grants administered by DoD, but relatively few respondents had experiences with grants other than those of Minerva and NSF.

The merit review criteria and evaluation process used for the Minerva solicitation in 2008 followed NSF procedures, which are similar to DoD's as just described (National Science Foundation, 2008). NSF sometimes encourages white papers, but this is not typically the case. Often, letters of intent are requested (as was the case in 2008), and these letters are used primarily to gain a sense of the number and content of the proposals being submitted to facilitate planning for the review panels and other logistics. NSF proposals are typically reviewed by ad hoc panels of mainly academic reviewers (in contrast with DoD's panels of reviewers, which, as noted, often include government civilians). NSF reviewers apply two main review criteria: "intellectual merit," which addresses the potential to advance knowledge, and "broader impacts," which denotes the potential to contribute to the attainment of desired societal outcomes. The review also includes attention to the plan for carrying out the proposed activities, as well as the qualifications of the individual or team that will execute the project and the adequacy of resources. Summary ratings with accompanying narratives developed by the reviewers are considered by the program officer, who manages the review and makes recommendations for funding.

Selecting Awardees

The panels reviewing the full proposals rank order the projects they consider fundable and send their recommendations to the Minerva program office, along with a summary of the strengths and weaknesses of all proposals reviewed and the degree of consensus among reviewers. The Minerva program office aggregates the reviews and recommendations of each panel for each topic area and produces a report of the results. Minerva program office staff then meet with OSD staff and the service branch program managers to make final decisions on which projects to fund and the level of funding. The 2018 grant announcement states that "the recommendations of the various area POCs [points of contact] will be forwarded to senior officials from the OSD who will make final funding recommendations to the awarding officials based on reviews, portfolio balance interests, and funds available" (Department of Defense Washington Headquarters Services/Acquisition Directorate, 2018, p. 23).

Awarding the Grants

Once sign-off on the list of grants to be funded has been received, the Minerva program office circulates the list of projects throughout DoD and sends award letters to the PIs who have been selected to receive a grant. As noted above, in 2018, proposals were due on August 14; the awards were then announced in January 2019. A letter is also sent to those who did not receive awards. The program managers from each service branch then follow up and implement the grants though their procurement offices. The proposals, recommendations, ratings, and assessments become part of the grant packages.

Once PIs have been informed that they will be funded, the program managers discuss with them expectations for their projects and any points of concern. A kick-off meeting is sometimes held, particularly for larger projects.

Some service branches require grantees to have human subjects research approval from their home institution and by the service branch's institutional review board (IRB) before a grant involving human subjects is awarded. A service branch's IRB may or may not accept the university's IRB approval, and this can contribute to a considerable delay in the transfer of funds.

Managing Grants and Monitoring Grant Progress and Performance

The 2018 grant announcement described three categories of expectations for Minerva researchers: project meetings and reviews, research output, and reporting requirements (Department of Defense Washington

Headquarters Services/Acquisition Directorate, 2018, p. 7). Project meetings and reviews include participation in the Minerva Conference, typically held annually in the Washington, DC, area; individual project reviews with the service branch sponsor; project status reviews focused on the latest research results and any other incremental progress; and interim meetings as needed. Research output includes expectations for products, publications, and analytical summaries of findings that can be shared with the government and others. Reporting requirements are for annual and final technical reports, financial reports, final patent reports, and copies of publications and presentations.

Because a grant is executed between the sponsoring service branch and the grantee's academic institution, the service branches manage the grants. OSD is not directly involved in grant management because it is not structured administratively to perform these types of functions. The Minerva program office obtains information about the status of awards, delays, and progress from the service branch program managers. The Minerva program office has no direct access to progress reports submitted to the service branches (all of which have different requirements and timelines). As discussed in Chapter 1, at the time of this writing, a centralized Minerva grants database was under development to help monitor grant funding and progress.

At the individual service branch level, various methods are used to monitor grant performance and progress. Some service branch program managers write to grantees immediately after their award to let them know what is expected of them, such as obtaining IRB approval, if needed; sending monthly invoices; and maintaining regular contact. Some program managers request to be informed about dissemination activities related to the project, such as briefings, interactions with the media, conference submissions, and awards. Some service branch program managers are able to monitor grantee spending rates more closely than others. ARO's approach was to conduct site visits for every grant at least once in the life cycle of 3- to 5-year grants. AFOSR and ONR convene their own annual program reviews, which tend to be weeklong events and include a review of Minerva grants—in the case of AFOSR, a subset of those grants, selected by the program manager on a rotating basis.

Each branch also has its own requirements and procedures for obtaining annual progress reports. Some send formal annual progress report forms to PIs with an automated request to complete them by the same date each year, regardless of when the grants started during the year. Some service branch program managers receive reports about which annual reports have been submitted and which are overdue. The forms used for progress reports vary across the branches.

NSF postaward reporting requirements are broadly similar to those of the DoD service branches. They include annual and final project reports with information on accomplishments, project participants, publications, other products, and impacts. Grantees are expected to monitor adherence to performance goals, time schedules, and other conditions of the grant. Contact between the NSF program officers and PIs is encouraged to address progress and changes in projects.

Supporting Dissemination Activities

Dissemination of the findings from Minerva research commonly occurs at the individual project level; some Minerva researchers are particularly well known in the national security community, publish a great deal, attend professional conferences, and are asked to provide briefings to various audiences on their projects. DoD facilitates several forms of dissemination, but staffing constraints in the Minerva program office limit such efforts, including dissemination about Minerva to the broader social science research community.

The annual Minerva Conference is a major dissemination venue where connections can be forged across research, policy, and national security communities. At the 2018 conference, an effort was made to highlight the National Defense Strategy and to generate more interaction between DoD policy staff and the Minerva researchers so as to showcase who is being funded and what is being learned.

Another avenue for dissemination is the Strategic Multilayer Assessment, a DoD organizational unit operated by the Joint Chiefs of Staff that sponsors a joint lecture series with the Minerva program. Minerva speakers are invited to speak on topics that address challenges faced by the Joint Chiefs.

Efforts also are under way to build the dissemination capacity of the Minerva Research Initiative website. These efforts include redesigning the website by (1) changing the URL to minerva.defense.gov to be less focused on the military (the previous web address was http://minerva.dtic.mil), (2) incorporating a series of social science blogs in which researchers will discuss their research to educate people on social science contributions to national security, and (3) adding information about all of the Minerva grants.

At the service branch level, dissemination often occurs through responses to calls for information on research findings from individuals or organizational units, such as special operations, training groups, or other DoD branches. Colloquium-like events where research can be proactively disseminated are being considered as another vehicle.

Supporting Translation Activities

Translation activities (also referred to as transition or transitional activities) are steps that can be taken to translate basic research to applied research. DoD defines basic research as "systematic study directed toward greater knowledge or understanding of the fundamental aspects of phenomena and of observable facts without specific applications towards processes or products in mind," and applied research as "systematic study to gain knowledge or understanding necessary to determine the means by which a recognized and specific need may be met" (Department of Defense, 2017). DoD refers to funding allocated for basic research, such as the Minerva grants, as 6.1 funding, and to the funding allocated for applied research as 6.2 funding. In 2018, the Minerva program office initiated a request for some 6.2 funding, but this request did not receive sufficient support to advance.

Service branch program managers sometimes promote the work of their grantees to other funders and refer them to other funding streams, including 6.2 grants, for follow-on research. Potential funders include the Department of Justice, the Department of Homeland Security, the Defense Advanced Research Projects Agency, and the Defense Threat Reduction Agency. Technical exchange meetings between PIs working on 6.1 and 6.2 projects within the service branches and between PIs and Central Command or Special Operations Command also facilitate translational activities.

In two cases, the results of Minerva research projects were advanced to 6.2 grants. These cases fell into an area of analytics that could be applied to open-source data and a variety of problems.

DISCUSSION OF MINERVA PROGRAM PROCESSES

The committee's evaluation of the Minerva program processes revealed opportunities for process improvements both to strengthen the program and to enhance the grantees' experiences.

Process Improvements to Strengthen the Program

A particularly challenging aspect of the Minerva program's organizational structure is the need to coordinate the interests of the policy office and the service branches. The two bring different perspectives to the Minerva collaboration, and the resulting tensions are understandably difficult to navigate. Policy makers typically need answers quickly and are accustomed to making decisions based on the information available at the time. By contrast, academic research—the focus of the research units within the service branches—involves investigating a question thoroughly before conclusions suitable to inform policy decisions are reached.

As discussed, these tensions lead in practice to challenges associated with the process of identifying research priorities (topics) and projects to fund in a given year. During the early years of the program, the views of the policy office carried more weight in the decision-making process relative to those of the service branches, and as a result, the service branches felt less invested in the Minerva program. To address this, the service branches were given a much more active role in recent years. It appears, however, that the shift came too late for ARO, which as noted, decided to withdraw from the partnership at the end of 2018 and will no longer participate in supporting new awards (the ARO program manager will continue to manage the existing ARO awards).

Based on the interviews with DoD staff, it appears that the service branch program managers are decidedly more satisfied with their role in the program under the current arrangement. It is important to note, however, that an emphasis on the types of basic research projects that the service branch research units consider a good fit for the program might be less satisfactory for DoD staff who are looking at the merits of the projects funded through the lens of their potential policy applications. In addition, DoD-wide priorities (represented by two of the topics funded in 2018, "Economic Interdependence and Security" and "Alliances and Burden-Sharing") are, by definition, broader than the topic areas of interest to the service branches.

It is too early to assess how well the new structure is functioning. There are no easy solutions that could result in a completely harmonious process, and it is likely that compromises will always be necessary. However, deepening the understanding of the Minerva Research Initiative and actively nurturing collaborations in support of the program across DoD divisions is essential. Changes in several areas, discussed below, could lead to a smoother process and a stronger program.

The Minerva program operates with a very small staff, and over the course of the past few years was overseen by an interim director who was able to dedicate only 20 percent of her time to the program. The current deputy director was brought on board as part of the Intergovernmental Personnel Act Mobility Program, which facilitates the temporary assignment of individuals from other organizations to government positions. The former interim director (and ARO program manager) served in the capacity of assistant director until ARO withdrew from the program. The service branch program managers oversee individual grants on behalf of their branches. (For further detail on the organizational structure of the Minerva program, see Chapter 1.)

Most of the changes identified by the committee as priorities for strengthening the Minerva program and improving its performance require the attention of a full-time leader, in a position designed for the long term. To ensure continuity and appropriate stature, the director needs to hold a civil service position at the GS-15 level (or higher) and have a relevant Ph.D. or equivalent experience with the types of research that are funded by the program. To implement the committee's recommendations for improving the program, the Minerva office might also need an additional staff person, such as a research assistant, or the ability to bring in help for specific tasks as needed.

> **RECOMMENDATION 3.1:** The Department of Defense should ensure that the Minerva Research Initiative has a leader with appropriate credentials and stature in a full-time, civil service position.

> **RECOMMENDATION 3.2:** The Department of Defense should evaluate what additional support staff are needed for the Minerva Research Initiative to achieve its goals and implement the recommendations in this report.

The committee identified two tasks that are high priorities going forward (Recommendations 3.3 and 3.4 below). The interviews conducted with DoD staff for this study made it clear that the Minerva program is not as well known within DoD as it could be, and its unique benefits are not well understood by all those in leadership positions across the divisions. Some of this lack of understanding is due to the challenges associated with the program's focus on basic research and the inherent lack of immediate policy applications. However, there is also a lack of general awareness within DoD and the broader national security community of what the program does, the specific projects that are funded, and the expertise of grantees.

While the aim of basic research is not to produce immediately usable policy insights, the Minerva grantees' work in particular geographic areas of the world on a variety of priority topics has yielded a wealth of knowledge that appears to be highly underutilized, based on the input received by the committee, and particularly through the interviews with DoD staff. That input and the committee's own observations showed that a small subset of the grantees actively promote their research, and their work is well known in some national security circles. In some cases, moreover, service branch program managers have been proactive in raising awareness of Minerva research, mostly as ad hoc activities involving specific projects. However, the committee also found that there has been no systematic focus to date on disseminating information about the research funded through the Minerva program or on providing opportunities for the grantees to interact with policy makers or others who might be interested in the work.

As discussed, DoD only recently began developing a centralized database of the grants that have been awarded as part of the Minerva Research Initiative. At the time of the committee's evaluation, there was no mechanism, other than word of mouth, for identifying relevant research or expertise, even when someone expressed an interest in consulting Minerva research or researchers on a particular topic. Therefore, as a first step toward broadening understanding of the program's benefits, the Minerva program office needs to prioritize the completion of this database. The database needs to be searchable and to include detailed information on the focus of each grantee's research and the researchers' areas of expertise. The value of the Minerva grants is not only in the research produced but also in the expertise of the researchers, and the database needs to enable the easy identification of relevant expertise whenever the need or opportunity arises for a briefing, input, or some other form of dissemination.

The database needs to be centralized, integrating information about all of the grants funded through the Minerva program from its inception, regardless of which service branch managed them. The database also needs to be widely accessible to everyone within DoD. A public-facing version of the database is needed as well, containing perhaps fewer administrative details about the grants, but sufficient information about the research and the expertise of the researchers to facilitate its broad use (see Chapter 5 and Recommendation 5.2).

> **RECOMMENDATION 3.3:** The Minerva program office should make completing the centralized database of the projects and researchers funded under the Minerva Research Initiative a high priority.

In addition to developing this database, another priority for the Minerva program office is to formulate a more proactive approach to building relationships with leadership across DoD and others who could benefit from learning about the grantees' work, both within the department and externally. Intentional outreach could not only increase the usefulness of the research produced under the program but also strengthen support for the program among stakeholders.

> **RECOMMENDATION 3.4:** The Minerva program office should develop relationships with potential supporters of the Minerva Research Initiative and users of the research, both among Department of Defense leadership and externally, to increase awareness of the program and expand use of its funded research and the expertise of its grantees.

Process Improvements to Enhance the Grantees' Experiences

Beyond improvements that would benefit all stakeholders in the Minerva program, the committee also identified improvements that would enhance the grantees' experience. The committee identified these opportunities primarily from the responses provided to the grantee survey and the survey of administrators of sponsored research at academic institutions (see Chapter 2).

Comparison of Minerva and Other Grant Programs

Generally speaking, the great majority of the grantees who have had experience with NSF grants in addition to DoD's Minerva grants reported being much more, somewhat more, or at least as satisfied with the characteristics of the Minerva program relative to the NSF grants (see Table 3-1). "Selection of important topics for research" stood out in particular as an area in which more than half of the grantee respondents were "much more" or "somewhat more" satisfied with Minerva grants than with NSF grants. However, it is important to note that some NSF funding opportunities do not specify predetermined topics as does the Minerva program, and that the thematic solicitations do not specifically target researchers focused on national security topics. This difference could explain why respondents to the grantee survey were particularly satisfied with the Minerva program in terms of the topic selection.

TABLE 3-1 Grantee Satisfaction with Aspects of the Minerva Program Compared with National Science Foundation Grants (percentages)

Aspect	Much/Somewhat Less Satisfied (%)	About the Same (%)	Much/Somewhat More Satisfied (%)	Unable to Compare This Aspect (%)
Selection of important topics for research	10	37	54	—
White paper process	12	32	37	20
Full proposal submission process and requirements	12	56	29	2
Communication during the proposal stage	12	51	34	2
Postaward grant management (e.g., incremental funding, modifications, no-cost extensions, compliance with terms and conditions)	15	54	24	7
Institutional review board requirements	22	56	12	10
Financial and narrative grant reporting requirements	15	68	17	2
Postaward communication	15	37	44	5
Assistance with dissemination or translation of research findings	7	56	22	15

NOTES: Sample size = 41. Grantee survey Q4: "How satisfied are you with the following aspects of the Minerva grant program compared to National Science Foundation grants?"

The IRB process was the area in which the highest proportion (22%) of grantees said they found the DoD process much less or somewhat less satisfactory than the NSF process, although the majority of the grantees described their satisfaction with DoD and NSF IRB processes as "about the same." The human subjects review process was also one of the most frequently noted challenges (mentioned by 12% of the grantees) when grantees were asked to list the challenges they face "in conducting unclassified research relevant to national security that are different from the challenges you face in conducting research in other areas."

Grantees were also asked to compare their experiences with the Minerva program and those with DHS grants and grants other than Minerva from the DoD service branches. Comparisons with DHS grants showed patterns similar to those for NSF grants, but the number of grantees who had experience with both Minerva and DHS grants was too small to permit meaningful conclusions (n = 9). Not surprisingly given the similarities, the majority of Minerva grantees who also had experience with other grants from the DoD service branches were about equally satisfied with the two programs; very few were less satisfied with Minerva. It is interesting that a little over one in three grantees (37%) said they were much more or somewhat more satisfied with the "selection of important topics for research" in the Minerva program relative to other grant programs run by the service branches. The number of responding grantees who had experience with both Minerva and other service branch grant programs and who were therefore able to make these comparisons was relatively small (n = 19), and grantees who have received a Minerva grant are only a subset of those who have had experience with other grants from the service branches. However, this finding may be an indication that despite the challenges involved in reconciling the priorities of different DoD stakeholders, the collaborative Minerva program produces similar or better results relative to other service branch grant programs from the perspective of grantees. For detailed survey results, see Appendix E.

As discussed in Chapter 2, the committee also conducted a survey of administrators of sponsored research. This survey produced somewhat different results from the grantee survey in terms of comparisons with other grant programs (see Appendix F for detailed results). The number of respondents to this survey who had experience working with the Minerva program was small (11 of 88 respondents who completed the survey), and because the committee anticipated this, respondents to the administrator survey were also asked to compare DoD grant programs in general with NSF and DHS grant programs.[1]

---

[1] The grantees were asked to compare their satisfaction with the grant programs, while the administrators of sponsored programs were asked to compare the extent to which various aspects of the grant programs were more or less challenging (see Appendixes E and F, respectively, for the wording of the questions).

TABLE 3-2 Comparison of Aspects of DoD Grant Programs in General and National Science Foundation Grants by Administrators of Sponsored Research

Aspect	Much/ Somewhat More Challenging (%)	About the Same (%)	Much/ Somewhat Less Challenging (%)	Unable to Compare This Aspect (%)	Skipped
Proposal submission process and requirements	75	14	5	6	—
Communication during the proposal stage	51	32	8	10	—
Postaward grant management (e.g., incremental funding, modifications, no-cost extensions, compliance with terms and conditions)	72	16	5	6	—
Financial and narrative reporting requirements	58	28	5	9	—
Postaward communication	56	30	4	9	1
Other award characteristics (e.g., indirect costs)	47	46	1	5	1

NOTES: Sample size = 79. Survey of administrators of sponsored research Q8: "How do the following aspects of DoD grant programs in general compare to NSF grants?"

In general, respondents to this survey were less likely than grantee respondents to compare aspects of the DoD grant process favorably with aspects of the NSF process. For example, 75 percent described the DoD proposal submission process and requirements as much more or somewhat more challenging relative to NSF grants, and 72 percent said the same about postaward grant management. Most respondents rated the key characteristics of DoD and DHS grants about the same. Tables 3-2 and 3-3, respectively, summarize the comparisons of DoD and NSF and DHS grants.

When asked about the changes they would like to see to the Minerva program, four respondents to the survey of administrators of sponsored research provided comments that indicated a need for increasing awareness about the program and providing additional detail on how the program works. In terms of changes to DoD grant programs in general, the most frequently volunteered open-ended responses were related to the standardization of procedures (reporting and administrative requirements) across the department's various grant programs and the need to improve the DoD online systems used for the management of the grants.

TABLE 3-3 Comparison of Aspects of DoD Grant Programs in General and Department of Homeland Security Grants by Administrators of Sponsored Research

Aspect	Much/Somewhat More Challenging (%)	About the Same (%)	Much/Somewhat Less Challenging (%)	Unable to Compare This Aspect (%)	Skipped
Proposal submission process and requirements	15	48	19	17	2
Communication during the proposal stage	11	56	11	20	2
Postaward grant management (e.g., incremental funding, modifications, no-cost extensions, compliance with terms and conditions)	15	54	13	17	2
Financial and narrative reporting requirements	13	52	13	20	2
Postaward communication	11	56	11	20	2
Other award characteristics (e.g., indirect costs)	9	59	11	19	2

NOTES: Sample size = 54. Survey of administrators of sponsored research Q9: "How do the following aspects of DoD grant programs in general compare to Department of Homeland Security grants?"

Human Subjects Review Requirements

One area in which changes would notably improve the grantee experience is the human subjects review process. Currently, studies often require approval by the IRBs of both the service branch managing the grant and the grantee's home institution. In the case of grants with more than one PI, several academic institutions may be involved. The service branches each have their own rules about the human subjects review process, and grantees are encouraged to work with the service branch program manager overseeing their project to navigate the process. AFOSR does not release funds until IRB approval has been obtained. Projects managed by ARO can receive funds that do not involve human subjects research prior to obtaining IRB approval for the portion of the work that involves data collection, and the ARO Human Research Protections Office reviews the IRB approval obtained by PIs from their academic institutions for compliance with ARO standards. ONR does not require separate review by the ONR

IRB either, and instead reviews the approval obtained by grantees from their own academic institution. This model imposes the least burden on the grantees while ensuring that the necessary human subjects protections are in place and providing DoD with an opportunity to identify any potential issues of concern.

In principle, NSF also requires IRB approval before an award is made, but exceptions are possible if preliminary work needs to take place before the research protocol has been finalized. In these cases, the grant can be set up in a way that permits some work, with the exception of data collection, to begin before IRB approval (National Science Foundation, 2014, p. II-30).

Information obtained from the interviews with DoD staff and the responses to the grantee survey suggest that the human subjects review procedures of some of the service branches place an extra burden on the grantees and delay the start of work. Perhaps this issue could be addressed by developing, to the extent feasible, common procedures that would apply to all Minerva grants, regardless of which service branch is overseeing them. A combination of the ONR, ARO, and NSF approaches could result in a reasonable compromise that would facilitate the grantees' work. Providing funding for some preliminary work that does not involve data collection prior to IRB approval appears especially reasonable.

The revisions to the Federal Policy for the Protection of Human Subjects (also known as the Common Rule) that began taking effect in 2018 and are being introduced in several phases require "U.S.-based institutions engaged in cooperative research to use a single IRB for that portion of the research that takes place within the United States."[2] This change appears to be applicable primarily to multisite projects, but the underlying intent is to reduce the overall challenges associated with navigating the review process for studies that require approval by multiple IRBs. DoD could also consider having one IRB of record for the Minerva grants.

> RECOMMENDATION 3.5: The Department of Defense (DoD) should reduce the burden and project delays associated with the human subjects review process for Minerva grants by using a single Institutional Review Board (IRB) of record for each grant. For example, the IRB of record could be that of the principal investigator's academic institution, with DoD reviewing that approval. DoD should also consider releasing funds prior to IRB approval for portions of the work that do not involve human subjects research.

---

[2] Available: https://www.govinfo.gov/content/pkg/FR-2017-01-19/pdf/2017-01058.pdf.

4

Research Supported by the Minerva Program: Quantity and Quality

This chapter reviews the research output that has been supported by Minerva grants. To gain an understanding of this research, the committee relied on the information sources described in Chapter 2, including Department of Defense (DoD) documents and interviews with DoD staff, the grantee survey, the sponsored research administrators survey, discussions with national security experts and other stakeholders at public committee meetings, and the Minerva Conference. The committee also analyzed the outputs reported by the Minerva grantees.

The first section of this chapter describes the committee's review and analysis of the grant outputs. The second section provides an overview of the perceptions of Minerva research among those who provided input to the committee. The chapter ends with a summary.

REVIEW OF OUTPUTS OF THE MINERVA RESEARCH INITIATIVE GRANTS

Assessment of research outputs often relies on both qualitative peer review and quantitative assessment using various types of bibliometric indicators (Hicks and Wouters, 2015; Moed, 2017). Strengths and weaknesses have been identified in both approaches (deRijcke et al., 2016; Siler et al., 2015), but it can be argued that peer review is the stronger method for evaluating the outputs of individual researchers and small research units, while quantitative bibliometrics are more useful in assessing the outputs of large and heterogeneous groups of researchers (Sugimoto and Lariviere, 2018). Because the committee's evaluation of the Minerva Research Initiative is targeted at the program level, it relies primarily on quantitative indicators to assess the program's research outputs while also considering input from stakeholders for additional context. The committee considered a variety of additional approaches and analyses for carrying out this task, but rejected them because of their limitations.

Accordingly, the committee's review of the outputs of Minerva-sponsored research involved compiling lists of the outputs, coding and summarizing the outputs by type and subtype, and examining in greater depth the journals in which articles were published and the citations of those articles by other researchers as an indicator of contributions to the social science knowledge base. The committee also considered outreach and dissemination to nonacademic audiences by reviewing nonacademic publications reported by Minerva principal investigators (PIs). As discussed in Chapter 2, one of the challenges for the evaluation was that the Minerva program had been in existence for less than 10 years at the time this study was launched, and many of the grants were relatively recent and/or still active. The evaluation results could thus be affected because such grants likely have produced fewer outputs and fewer citations of their publications relative to grants initiated earlier.

Output Data and Coding

As part of the committee's grantee survey, grantees were asked to provide lists of their Minerva-sponsored outputs, which included peer-reviewed publications, any other publications (e.g., papers, manuscripts, reports, op-ed pieces), presentations (e.g., conference presentations, briefings, or testimony); and any other products, such as publicly available software, websites, databases, patents, licenses, or training materials that resulted from their Minerva grant(s) (for details, see Chapter 2 and Appendix E).

As discussed in Chapter 2, to facilitate response to the survey, grantees could submit information about their outputs by either responding to the survey questions or uploading their curriculum vitae (CV), highlighting outputs that resulted from their Minerva grant. The survey questions asked about "peer-reviewed publications" and "other publications" (see Appendix E, Q17 and Q18). However, in the case of grantees who chose to upload a CV, this distinction often was unknown. Therefore, the peer-reviewed status of all journal publications was ascertained according to three library databases: Scopus, Proquest, and Ulrich's.

The definitions of peer review used by these three sources are quite broad. Scopus, for example, defines peer review as including various strategies, such as main editor peer review, open peer review, single-blind peer review, and double-blind peer review (Scopus, 2019a,f). To designate journals as peer-reviewed, Proquest uses Ulrich's (Ulrich's Web, n.d.), which uses the term "refereed" for such journals. Ulrich's website states, "Refereed serials include articles that have been reviewed by experts and respected researchers in specific fields of study including the sciences, technology, the social sciences, and arts and humanities" (Ulrich's Web, n.d.). It is possible, moreover, that some articles counted by the committee as being published in a peer-reviewed journal may actually have been review or opinion articles that may not have been peer-reviewed. Additionally, rules for which types of articles are peer-reviewed vary across journals. For example, the website of *Nature Research* states that the journal subjects articles, letters, brief communications, technical reports, analyses, resources, reviews, perspectives, and insight articles to peer review, while the website of the journal *International Organization* states that it sends all submissions, except letters to the editor, to reviewers. In addition, some journals (e.g., the *New England Journal of Medicine*) include articles that are invited but may not be peer-reviewed. The committee did not carry out a more refined assessment of the peer-review policies of different journals (i.e., searching each journal's website to identify which types of articles were peer-reviewed).

Finally, although books and conference proceedings may also be considered to be peer-reviewed, the committee limited the designation of peer-reviewed status for this evaluation to journals. This was primarily because standard library databases, such as Scopus (2019a) and Web of Science (Testa, 2017; Web of Science, 2019), cover limited types of books and conference proceedings; thus they could not be used to check the peer-reviewed status of all the books and conference proceedings reported by PIs. Appendix H describes additional coding procedures for publications and other types of outputs.

Number of Grantees Who Provided Information on Outputs

As reported in Chapter 2, 67 PIs provided information on outputs related to their Minerva grants. Four of these PIs stated that they were at a point too early in their grant to have produced outputs. Therefore, the following results pertain to information on outputs provided by 63 PIs. Six of these PIs reported only "other products" (i.e., publicly available software, websites, databases, patents, licenses, or training materials), but no publications or presentations. Therefore, the following summary of reported publications and presentations includes information from 57 PIs. This summary is followed by information on other products.

Summary of Minerva-Sponsored Publications and Presentations Reported by Principal Investigators

Table 4-1 provides a summary of the publications and presentations reported by PIs responding to the grantee survey. As discussed, the committee did not receive lists of outputs from all PIs, so the table represents a subset

TABLE 4-1 Summary of Publications and Presentations Reported by Principal Investigators (PIs)

	All 57 PI Reports				Nonzero PI Reports		
Output Type	Number of Outputs	Percent of All Outputs	Range	Median	Total (Percent of 57)	Range	Median
Publications							
Peer-reviewed publications	152	13	0–18	2	39 (68%)	1–18	3
Other, non-peer-reviewed publications	333	28	0–124	1	36 (63%)	1–124	2.5
Books and book chapters	62	5	0–12	0	21 (37%)	1–12	1
Conference proceedings	28	2	0–18	0	5 (9%)	1–18	3
Publications in progress	47	4	0–7	0	17 (30%)	1–7	2
Presentations	582	48	0–80	5	44 (77%)	1–80	8
Total Publications and Presentations	1,204	100%	1–133	10	57 (100%)	1–133	10

of all Minerva grants. (See Chapter 2 for further detail on this and other limitations of data on Minerva outputs obtained from the grantee survey.) Despite limitations of the data, the committee's focus on relatively more robust measures (such as medians and percentages rather than means and totals) should ensure that the analyses and conclusions concerning the outputs from Minerva grants are reasonably robust.

Columns 2 and 3 of Table 4-1 show the numbers of publications and presentations produced by Minerva grantees by type, and for each type, the proportion of the total reported by the 57 PIs who provided this information. Slightly more than half of all the outputs (52%) reported by these PIs consisted of written materials in the form of peer-reviewed journal publications, other publications, books or book chapters, and conference proceedings; the other half (48%) was presentations, including briefings and testimony. Columns 4 and 5 of Table 4-1 show the range and median number of each type of publication and presentation reported across the 57 PIs. The ranges are quite wide, and some output categories (other, non-peer-reviewed publications and conference proceedings) are dominated by one extraordinarily productive grantee.

Columns 6 through 8 of the table present the same information without the PIs who reported no outputs in certain categories. While funding studies that ultimately lead to no outputs would be a concern, examining this additional information about the distribution of outputs is useful because as noted, some of the grants included in the evaluation were in the very early stages after being awarded, and some were focused primarily on producing the types of outputs that are not included in this table. When PI observations that were zero are excluded (Column 6), slightly higher medians are seen in Column 8. For example, whereas the median for peer-reviewed publications is two when all 57 PIs are counted, the median is 3 when only observations for PIs with at least one peer-reviewed publication are used (68% of the 57 PIs reported one or more peer-reviewed publication).

Whereas Table 4-1 provides summary data for all publications and presentations reported by all responding PIs, Table 4-2 provides summaries, by year of the PI's grant (2009 to 2017), for all publications/presentations (Columns 2–4) and for the subset of peer-reviewed publications (Column 5–7). The pattern of outputs is generally in the expected direction over time, from higher numbers produced in earlier years (except the initial startup years, 2009 and 2010) to lower numbers produced in more recent years, reflecting the more limited time available to recent grantees to publish and give presentations. This same general pattern can be seen in Appendix I, which provides a similar view of the range and median of each type of publication and presentation, broken out by year of the grant.

TABLE 4-2 Summary of All Publications and Presentations and Peer-Reviewed Journal Publications, by Year of Grant, Reported by Principal Investigators (PIs)

Year of Grant (No. of PIs Reporting)	All Publications and Presentations			Peer-Reviewed Publications		
	Number	Range	Median	Number	Range	Median
2009 (3)	236	1–124	111	18	0–18	0
2010 (12)	129	1–30	8	30	0–5	2.5
2012 (5)	237	9–133	24	16	0–5	4
2013 (7)	187	16–37	26	36	0–15	5
2014 (8)	189	3–45	20.5	20	0–7	2
2015 (10)	113	2–32	7.5	24	0–6	2
2016 (7)	87	2–52	6	4	0–2	0
2017 (5)	26	1–9	6	4	0–4	0
Total All Years (57)	1204	1–133	10	152	0–18	2

Journal-Level Impact Metrics for Peer-Reviewed Publications Reported by Principal Investigators

Journal-level impact metrics can be used to assess the quality and influence of journals, but some approaches to constructing such metrics and some uses of the metrics have been criticized (Agarwal et al., 2016; Sugimoto and Lariviere, 2018). It has been argued, for example, that calculating citations over only a 2-year period, as is the case for some metrics, provides inadequate time for such a field as the social sciences to accrue citations. Journal impact metrics also have been used inappropriately to assess individual researchers even though they were developed as journal-level indicators.

Although all journal-level impact metrics have limitations, two with relatively strong measurement properties are CiteScore and the Scimago Journal Ranking (SJR) (González-Pereira et al., 2010; James et al., 2018; Sugimoto and Lariviere, 2018). A journal's CiteScore for 2017, for example, counts the citations made in 2017 to documents published by the journal in the previous 3 years (2014, 2015, or 2016), and divides the total number of citations by the number of documents published by the journal in those same years (Scopus, 2019d). The SJR divides the weighted number of citations received in a year by the number of documents published in the previous 3 years. The weights are intended to reflect the prestige of the journals in which the citations appear (Scopus, 2019e).

Consistent with recommendations in the literature to use multiple indicators (Hicks and Wouters, 2015; Moed, 2017), the committee gathered both CiteScore and SJR metrics for journals in which Minerva researchers published. These metrics were accessed through the National Academies' research library via the Scopus database, which is considered to have wider coverage than Web of Science, including good coverage of the social sciences (Sugimoto and Lariviere, 2018). The committee used CiteScore and SJR as journal-level indicators only, not to assess individual researchers.

The detailed results of these metrics for 112 journals in which the 57 Minerva PIs reported publishing are provided in two appendix tables. The table in Appendix J1 shows the CiteScore and SJR metrics for 82 peer-reviewed journals. The table in Appendix J2 lists the remaining 30 of the 112 journals, for which CiteScore and SJR journal-level metrics were not available. Of these 30 journals, 12 were found to be peer-reviewed according to the designation explained earlier, while 18 were found not to be peer-reviewed. Impact factor metrics may not be available for journals because they are not designated as peer-reviewed, are too new to have established data for calculating journal impact factors, or do not meet criteria for being included in the major library citation indexes that feed into the CiteScore or SJR databases. Columns 1 and 2 of both appendix tables list the journal names and the number of Minerva-sponsored articles published in each. Across the 82 journals for which CiteScore and SJR metrics were available (presented in Appendix J1), 138 Minerva-supported articles were published, based on the data available to the committee from the grantee survey. Column 3 of Table J1 contains for each journal a subject field to which it is assigned by Scopus (Scopus, 2019g). Columns 4–6 (shaded) contain three metrics based on CiteScore: (1) the 2017 CiteScore, (2) a rank that allows for comparing journals *within* a subject field (e.g., 4/1029 means that a journal's citation impact ranks 4th out of 1,029 journals in that journal's subject field), and (3) a percentile that allows for comparing journals *across* subject fields[1] (Scopus, 2019c). Columns 7–9 (unshaded) of Table J1 contain three similar SJR metrics. Instead of percentiles, SJR calculates quartiles, with Q1 being the highest. The same subject fields used to gather CiteScore metrics were used to gather SJR metrics. The table is sorted, first, by the CiteScore percentile, from highest percentile (99th) to lowest, and then alphabetically by the journal name.

Table 4-3 summarizes the CiteScore and SJR rankings for the journals in which the 138 articles produced by Minerva-supported grants were published, displaying the number of articles for each combination of CiteScore decile and SJR quartile. The table shows that 46 percent (63 of 138) of the articles reported by PIs were published in journals that fell into the top CiteScore decile and the top SJR quartile. Another 29 percent (40 of 138) fell into the second or third CiteScore decile and the top SJR quartile. These findings reveal that articles resulting from Minerva-supported grants have been published in top-ranked journals.

Table 4-4 shows the journal rankings for articles produced by Minerva-supported grantees when the articles are sorted into 13 subject fields.[2] The field with the most articles—53—is political science and international rela-

---

[1] According to Scopus (2019c), "CiteScore Percentile indicates the relative standing of a serial title in its subject field. The Percentile and Ranking are relative to a specific Subject Area." In displaying percentiles, Scopus first shows the subject area in which the source performed the best, and in some cases it also displays other subject fields in which the journal performed second, third, or fourth best. For its evaluation, the committee used the percentile for the area in which the journal performed the best, except in three cases in which that area did not appear to reflect most closely the goals of the journal. For example, *Public Choice* was rated highest in the area of sociology and political science, but the journal emphasizes economics as its dominant subject area, so the second-highest percentile, in the field of economics and econometrics, was used.

[2] In some cases, similar fields with only one journal were combined to form larger subject field groups. For example, the following eight subject fields that each have one or two journals were combined into one collapsed subject field called computer science, engineering, and mathematics: computer graphics and design, computer science application, general computer science, media technology, control and optimization, control and systems engineering, electrical and electronic engineering, and applied mathematics.

TABLE 4-3 Journal Rankings for Minerva-Supported Articles

	Number of Articles					
	Scimago Journal Ranking (SJR) Quartile					
CiteScore Percentile	Q1	Q2	Q3	Q4	Total	Row Percentage[a]
90–99	63	0	0	0	63	46
80–89	28	9	0	0	37	27
70–79	12	4	3	0	19	13
60–69	2	2	0	0	4	3
50–59	0	7	2	0	9	7
40–49	1	1	1	0	3	2
30–39	0	0	0	0	0	0
20–29	0	0	0	1	1	1
10–19	0	0	0	2	2	1
0–9	0	0	0	0	0	0
Total	106	23	6	3	138	100
Column Percentage[b]	77	17	4	2	100	

[a]Row total ÷ 138.
[b]Column total ÷ 138.

tions. Of the articles in that field, 55 percent were published in journals ranked in the top CiteScore decile, while 89 percent and 91 percent, respectively, were published in journals ranked in the top quartile according to CiteScore and SJR. The table also reveals considerable variety in the subject fields of the journals in which articles produced by Minerva-supported grantees have been published—consistent with the intent of the Minerva Research Initiative to support interdisciplinary research.

Article-Level Impact Metrics for Peer-Reviewed Publications Reported by Principal Investigators

In addition to the quality of journals in which Minerva researchers have published, the research can be assessed by examining the extent to which grantees' publications are cited in the work of other researchers. As observed by Sugimoto and Lariviere (2018, p. 64), "For the past few decades scholarly impact has been defined as an effect upon the scientific community, as measured through citations." Hicks and Melkers (2013) point to various theoretical interpretations of how citation counts measure scholarly impact (e.g., as a measure of importance, intellectual influence,

TABLE 4-4 Journal Rankings for Minerva-Supported Articles, by Subject Field

Journal Subject Field (number of journals)	Number of Articles	CiteScore Top Decile N	CiteScore Top Decile %	CiteScore Top Quartile N	CiteScore Top Quartile %	SJR Top Quartile N	SJR Top Quartile %
Political Science & International Relations (n = 23)	53	29	55	47	89	48	91
Sociology & Political Science (n = 11)	15	10	67	14	93	13	87
Computer Science, Engineering, Mathematics (n = 9)	9	5	56	7	78	8	89
General Social Sciences, General Arts & Humanities, Multidisciplinary, Development (n = 8)	12	4	33	9	75	8	67
Demography (n = 5)	6	2	33	6	100	6	100
Law (n = 5)	12	6	50	10	83	9	75
Psychology, Health (n = 5)	5	4	80	5	100	5	100
Anthropology and Cultural Studies (n = 4)	4	0	0	1	25	0	0
Management Related, Public Administration (n = 4)	5	0	0	2	40	4	80
History (n = 2)	2	0	0	1	50	1	50
Economics (n = 2)	4	1	17	1	17	1	17
General Sciences (Agriculture, Biology, Earth, Planet) (n = 2)	2	1	50	2	100	2	50
Religious Studies (n = 2)	9	1	11	9	100	1	11
All Fields	138	63	46	114	83	106	77

NOTE: SJR = Scimago Journal Ranking.

or authoritativeness). They suggest that the field has converged in viewing citations as an indicator of impact through their "social and cognitive influence on subsequent research" (p. 7). According to these authors, analyses of citations should include normalization that accounts for subject field and year of publication, and the results should be summarized using percentile distributions.[3] With such an approach, "analysts compare the actual citation counts to the rate to be expected" (Hicks and Melkers, 2013, p. 9) and are more likely to make correct assessments and fair comparisons (Bornnman and Marx, 2013).

Taking this approach, the committee used Scopus to obtain three article-level metrics: (1) counts of the number of citations for every article published by a Minerva grantee; (2) "benchmarked percentiles that show how citations received by each document compared with the average for similar documents, relative to a certain subject field" (Scopus, 2019b); and (3) the field-weighted citation impact (FWCI) metric, which is the "ratio of the total citations actually received to the total citations that would be expected based on the average of the subject field over a three-year window. A value greater than 1.00 means the document is more cited than expected according to the average" (Scopus, 2019b).

Appendix K presents a table of the results for each of 125 reported peer-reviewed Minerva publications for which article-level metrics could be found in Scopus,[4] sorted by the benchmarking percentile, from high to low. Of these 125 publications reported by Minerva PIs, 20 had zero or one citation, in some cases probably because the article had been published very recently or was still forthcoming; these articles had FWCIs equal to zero. The median FWCI of the 125 articles was 1.9. This implies that the median Minerva-sponsored publication has been cited more often than expected relative to the global average of 1.0. Indeed, about two-thirds (85) of the 125 Minerva publications for which this information was available had an FWCI exceeding 1.0.

With regard to the percentiles, percentiles relative to subject fields were not assigned by Scopus for 22 of the 105 articles with nonzero FWCIs.[5] The remaining 83 articles are presented first in the table in Appendix K, sorted by percentile, in descending order. Of these, 29 percent fell in the highest decile (the 90th–99th percentile), 66 percent fell in the highest quartile (75th–99th percentile), and 86 percent were above the median, relative to their subject fields. These percentages are shown in Table 4-5, which provides a cross-tabulation of the Minerva articles by FWCI and benchmarking

---

[3] Personal communication with Diana Hicks, March 25, 2019.

[4] Journal-level metrics (CiteScore and SJR) were gathered from Scopus for journals in which 138 Minerva-supported articles had been published. However, the article-level metrics reported in this section could be found in Scopus for only 125 articles. The metrics for the remaining 13 articles could be missing for varied reasons (e.g., a published article title may have been somewhat different from that reported on the grantee survey).

[5] Scopus explains that "citation benchmarking takes into account: (a) the date of publication, (b) the document type, and (c) disciplines associated with its source. Citation benchmarking compares articles within an 18 month window and is computed separately for each of its sources' disciplines. The Citation Benchmarking only appears when compared to all three criteria. A minimum set of 500 similar articles are required" (Scopus, 2019b).

percentile. The table also shows how the 22 articles with nonzero FWCIs but no assigned percentiles were distributed across FWCI categories.

Table 4-6 compares article-level benchmarking percentiles with journal-level CiteScore percentiles for the 83 articles for which both of these metrics were available. Twenty-two percent (18) of the 83 articles ranked in the top decile on both metrics, suggesting they were published in high-quality

TABLE 4-5 Summary of Article-Level Metrics for Minerva-Supported Articles

Benchmarking Percentile	Number of Articles						Row Percentage (excluding not assigned)[a]
	Field-Weighted Citation Impact						
	≥ 5	≥ 2, < 5	≥ 1, < 2	> 0, < 1	= 0	Total	
90–99	15	9	0	0	0	24	29
75–89	1	18	11	1	0	31	37
50–74	0	3	6	7	0	16	19
30–49	0	0	1	11	0	12	14
Not Assigned	9	6	6	1	20	42	–
Total	25	36	24	20	20	125	100
Column Percentage[b]	20	29	19	16	16	100	

[a]Row total ÷ 83.
[b]Column total ÷ 125.

TABLE 4-6 Comparison of Article Impacts and Journal Rankings for Minerva-Supported Articles

Article-level Benchmarking Percentile	Number of Articles						Row Percentage[a]
	Journal-Level CiteScore Percentile						
	90–99	75–89	50–74	30–49	<30	Total	
90–99	18	4	2	0	0	24	29
75–89	17	13	1	0	0	31	37
50–74	4	9	3	0	0	16	19
30–49	6	1	5	0	0	12	15
Total	45	27	11	0	0	83	100
Column Percentage[b]	54	33	13	0	0		100
Number Not Assigned a Benchmarking Percentile	18	24	7	3	3	55	

[a]Row total ÷ 83.
[b]Column total ÷ 83.

journals and had an impact on other researchers, as reflected by citations. Sixty-three percent (52) of the articles were in the top quartiles of both rankings. The table shows some tendency for articles to be ranked higher on the journal-level metric than on the article-level metric.

Outreach and Dissemination to Nonacademic Audiences

As noted in the earlier section summarizing the publications and presentations reported by PIs, in addition to 152 peer-reviewed academic publications and 582 presentations, Minerva PIs reported 333 other publications that included non-peer-reviewed journal articles, working papers, paper series, research briefs, commentaries and op-ed pieces, blogs, and newsletters. At least some of these publications appear to represent outreach and dissemination efforts aimed at nonacademic audiences to build public understanding of Minerva-supported research and highlight its policy implications. These publications appeared in a wide array of sources, such as *The New York Times, The Washington Post, Foreign Affairs Snapshots, Scientific American, The Atlantic, Cipher Brief, The Wire, McLeans, The National Interest*, and *Politico*, as well as international publications. Subject areas encompassed the breadth of Minerva grants since 2008 (see Appendix C for a list of grant titles). Examples of the subject areas covered are

- uniting warring armies after civil war;
- coups, elections, and the state of democracies;
- the new dictators: threats, fears, and personalism;
- humanitarian crises and refugee assistance;
- cyberdeterrence, command, security, response, and partnerships;
- the influence of world powers on developing or warring nations;
- managing versus resolving conflicts;
- what pirates want and where they strike;
- terrorist groups, how they communicate, and female extremists; and
- the weaponization of children.

Other Minerva-Sponsored Products Reported by Principal Investigators

This section describes other types of outputs and sharable resources reported by Minerva grantees, such as software, maps and mapping tools, websites, databases, patents and licenses, training materials, and models/methodologies. Thirty-three PIs reported developing a total of 85 such other products during the course of their Minerva grants. Box 4-1 provides an overview of the wide variety of the products developed, which might be as important, or more important than publications. The list is not exhaustive.

BOX 4-1
Other Products Developed through the
Minerva Research Initiative

Software

- Analytic software based on social network analysis, involving natural language processing, geospatial analysis, and machine learning
- Publicly available software for tracking online social movements, with applications for different countries

Mapping Tools

- A mapping tool that allows users to visualize data on climate change vulnerability, conflict, and aid to assess how climate change impacts and responses intersect
- An online, interactive mapping tool providing policy makers with a platform to visualize trends in climate-related disaster vulnerability, conflict, governance challenges, and disaster aid
- A tool for mapping extremist and counterextremist online narratives

Websites

- Content on complex emergencies and political stability
- Content on climate change and political stability
- Content on cyber international relations
- Cyber-related content and sustainable development
- A website mapping militants and militant groups
- Websites covering transportation networks, land cover, settlements, land rights, land use, land tenure, toponyms, and population

Databases

- An events-based dataset on social conflicts
- A dataset on armed conflict locations and events
- A geocoded climate dataset
- Education and infrastructure access data
- A constitutional design database
- A database on interstate and civil war termination
- A dataset on autocratic regimes
- Data on personalism in dictatorships
- A database on maritime piracy events and locations
- Climate and disaster aid data
- Disaster response training data
- Major episodes of mass nonviolent, violent, and "mixed" contentions

continued

BOX 4-1 Continued

Patents and Licenses

- A visual intelligence platform for tracking online social movements
- A system and method for contextual analysis
- Methods for determining the similarity of content and structuring unstructured content from heterogeneous sources
- Systems and methods for narrative and frame detection using generalized concepts and relations

Training Materials

- Climate change and development
- Institutional capacity and natural disasters
- Constitutional reform for conflict management
- Climate change and national security
- Languages across cultures

Models and Methodologies

- A climate security vulnerability model combining data on physical, socioeconomic, demographic, and political insecurities
- A climate disaster aid transparency codebook
- A climate security vulnerability model that identifies subnational locations most vulnerable to climate-related hazards, defined in terms of the potential for large-scale loss of life
- A topic modeling evaluation tool
- A language cohesion social media tool
- A sensitive data encoder
- A visual intelligence platform for tracking online social movements, with potential applications to programming more effectively, detecting and characterizing adversarial influence operations, analyzing the tactics of propaganda and disinformation, and tracking and refuting disinformation
- An algorithm to inform a K-means algorithm for prototype move selection in a simulation

STAKEHOLDER AND EXPERT PERCEPTIONS OF THE QUALITY OF MINERVA RESEARCH

In addition to its analysis of the outputs generated by the Minerva grants, the committee reached out to a broad range of stakeholders and national security experts and solicited input on the Minerva program through a public comment mechanism in an effort to better understand perceptions of the program's contributions to social science research on national security issues. These views are undeniably subjective, but they provide useful context for and an additional dimension to the bibliometric data reported above.

There appears to be broad agreement among both DoD staff and external stakeholders who provided input at the committee's public meetings that the Minerva Research Initiative is a unique program, and that the Minerva grants have attracted some top scholars and produced some high-quality research. In recent years, the program has struggled with staffing challenges, which have resulted in delayed postings of the grant announcement and a corresponding decline in the number of white papers submitted (the number of white papers was 313 in 2016, 261 in 2017, and 192 in 2018). However, Minerva staff reported a gradual increase in the quality of the proposals received over the years.

Some of the Minerva program managers noted that many Minerva grantees have been particularly productive, and that the quality of their branch's Minerva portfolio has been stronger than, or at least as strong as, that of the top grants funded through other programs within their branch. DoD senior leadership described the feedback they received about the Minerva research from both DoD staff and the broader national security community as indicating that the research has been well done, useful, and relevant. In a historical overview of the role of academic social science research in national security, Desch (2019, p. 236) observes that "Minerva attracted widespread interest among some leading social scientists." Box 4-2 highlights projects that have been described by Minerva leadership as being among the studies shaping social science research on national security. A full list of all of the Minerva funded projects is included in Appendix C.

At the same time, current and former DoD staff acknowledged that some of the projects funded by the program over the years have failed to meet DoD's expectations. The reasons cited ranged from poorly formulated research questions to structural challenges (for example, some grants were too large to operate efficiently). As discussed in Chapter 3, Minerva award decisions are often based on a negotiation that balances the goals of basic research and policy relevance, as well as the goals of the service branches and others within DoD. The DoD interviews suggested that in some cases, perceived policy relevance was the consideration that tipped the argument in favor of funding specific projects, and some have argued that this is the main reason why some projects fell short on scientific merit and the quality of the research. Other DoD staff expressed the view that the best way to make the program more useful would be to increase the policy relevance of projects, although they acknowledged that this is not the primary mission of the program.

> **BOX 4-2**
> **Examples of Minerva Projects Described
> by DoD as Shaping Social Science Research
> Relevant to National Security**
>
> - Terrorism, Governance, and Development: analysis of micro-level data on conflict using game-theoretic approaches to study nonviolent social systems (led to the establishment of the ongoing Empirical Studies of Conflict Project)
> - Spatio-Temporal Game Theory and Real Time Machine Learning for Adversarial Groups in the Wild: combining deep ethnography, psychology, and systems engineering to study gang decision-making in situ
> - Africa's Youth Bulge and National Security: mixed-methods approach to comprehensive study of Africa's youth bulge
> - Dynamics of Common Knowledge on Social Networks: online experimentation to study collective action and emergence of shared knowledge about events
> - Assessing the International Risk to National Economies Posed by a Marine Chokepoint Shutdown: modeling of complex interconnectedness
> - Political Reform, Socio-Religious Change, and Stability in the African Sahel: center and interdisciplinary approach to regional study
> - Deterrence with Proxies: behavioral economics and political modeling of proxy dynamics
> - Integrating Structural Theories of Revolution with Evolutionary Models to Predict Societal Resilience and (In)Stability: integrating social science and non–social science theories of revolution and resilience to examine questions of stability
> - Multi-Source Assessment of State Stability: mixed-methods, multimodeling approach used to support theory development and model validation to understand the role of a cyber-mediated environment and predict social stability
> - Complex Emergencies and Political Stability in Asia: quantitative and qualitative methods to explore insecurities that impact disaster vulnerability and complex emergencies, as well as strategies for response
> - Motivation, Ideology, and the Social Process in Radicalization and Deradicalization: social, cultural, and psychological approaches to analyzing the environment of radicalization
>
> SOURCE: Montgomery (2019).

Considering the unique contributions of the Minerva program, national security experts remarked that the program has been successful in facilitating interdisciplinary research. One perspective voiced by DoD staff was that the small but interdisciplinary and well-funded Minerva grants are a good example of the future of team science as an alternative to large, multidisciplinary, multi-institution research centers. Another DoD staff perspective was that Minerva projects are successful representations of a DoD-wide focus on such research areas as radicalization, stability and resilience, and geopolitical factors, in contrast to the somewhat narrower focus of other social science research programs in the service branches.

National security experts were generally in agreement that the Minerva program has remained true to its vision and objectives over the years. Given the relatively broad scope of the topics prioritized in the funding of projects, they did not raise specific concerns about those topics, but encouraged enough consistency from year to year to allow for a body of knowledge to develop.

With respect to ensuring that the benefits of the funded research are maximized, national security experts encouraged greater outreach, both within and outside of DoD, to communicate about the research and its results and to better understand stakeholder needs. Some examples provided of communities that could benefit from the research were foreign service officers and military academies. The theme of greater outreach was echoed by representatives of professional associations, who urged greater outreach from the Minerva program to their memberships.

SUMMARY AND CONCLUSIONS

The committee's ability to evaluate systematically all the products of the Minerva grants over the years was limited, and there was no group that could have served as a valid hypothetical comparison group for the volume and quality of the outputs produced by the Minerva grantees. It is clear, however, that the Minerva program has supported research that has been published in top journals and articles that have been cited much more than the average expected of their respective social science fields. In addition to peer-reviewed publications and presentations at academic conferences, Minerva researchers reported outreach and dissemination to nonacademic audiences through research briefs, commentaries, and other publications on the context, meaning, and implications of their research. While journals focused on political science and international relations had the highest number of publications based on Minerva research, Minerva research has been published in journals representing all major social science fields, and other fields, such as computer science, engineering, and mathematics. The diversity of journals that have published Minerva research illustrates the program's interdisciplinary nature. Likewise, the broad range of policy-relevant products and tools developed, such as software, maps and mapping tools, websites, databases, patents and licenses, training materials, and models/methodologies, indicates that the program values innovative outputs, beyond publications and conference presentations.

The input received from stakeholders and national security experts highlighted that the Minerva Research Initiative is a unique program and that its grants have attracted some top scholars and produced some high-quality research that is useful and relevant. The Minerva program has remained true to its vision, funding research that addresses social science questions of interest to all of DoD and the broader national security community. However, the input the committee received from national security experts, professional associations, and DoD staff indicated that the research is not as widely disseminated or utilized as it could be. Further discussion of this issue and the committee's recommendations for addressing it are included in Chapters 3 and 5.

5

Direction and Vision of the Minerva Program

This chapter addresses several of the research questions formulated by the committee that cut across various topic areas in the committee's charge (see Table 1-3 in Chapter 1). Specifically, the chapter addresses ways to make better use of Minerva research and researchers, changes that may be needed to Minerva's vision and goals, and opportunities for increasing social scientists' engagement with the program. Also discussed is the importance of developing benchmarks to enable continuous monitoring and evaluation.

MAKING BETTER USE OF MINERVA RESEARCH AND RESEARCHERS

Over the past decade, Minerva grants have produced a substantial body of research in a variety of areas of importance to national security. Respondents to the committee's survey of grantees (see Chapter 2) overwhelmingly reported that the program has had a positive impact on the amount of dialogue between the Department of Defense (DoD) and the social science community, the number of social science researchers with an interest in research relevant to national security, and the amount of collaboration among researchers working on a variety of national security topics (see Table 5-1). Based on the committee's interviews with DoD staff and the committee's own observations, however, the research is not utilized to maximum benefit because dissemination and outreach efforts have not yet been maximized.

It is important to note that dissemination is not a linear process. The research community becomes oriented to a policy area by listening to and

TABLE 5-1 Grantees' Perceptions of the Impact of Minerva Grants (percentages)

Area of Impact	Positive Impact	No Impact	Negative Impact	Unable to Say
The amount of dialogue between DoD and the social science research community as a whole	87	5	—	8
The number of social science researchers with interest in national security research	82	8	—	11
The amount of collaboration among researchers working on different national security research topics	76	11	—	13

NOTES: Sample size = 76; Grantee survey Q12: "Would you say the Minerva grant program has had a positive impact, no impact, or a negative impact on each of the following . . . ?"

participating in policy discussions involving policy makers and others. Researchers contribute to the body of knowledge on a continuous basis, and these resources become available to the broader community. Policy makers then can tap into the specific research directly, or can utilize the broader expertise of the researchers who have produced the body of knowledge. Those activities can stimulate further research that broadens both the body of knowledge and the expertise of researchers.

Going forward, it is essential to develop a systematic outreach and dissemination plan that is based on a carefully considered strategy to ensure that Minerva researchers are exposed to policy discussions and that the knowledge gained through Minerva research can benefit the broader national security community. This plan needs to include an approach for building institutionalized mechanisms that will facilitate the spread of information about the grants and is specifically targeted to the audiences the Minerva program office wants to reach, both within DoD and externally.

RECOMMENDATION 5.1: The Minerva program office should develop a strategic outreach and dissemination plan for distributing information about the Minerva Research Initiative and about the studies and researchers funded.

In addition to encouraging the development of a dissemination and outreach plan, the committee suggests several actions for the near term focused on increasing both the use of Minerva research and the expertise of the researchers, as detailed below.

When asked about opportunities for interaction with various national security staff and policy makers, the majority of the grantees responding to the committee's survey said that the Minerva program had increased ("greatly" or "somewhat") opportunities for these types of interaction with service branch staff interested in integrating basic research insights into their work (68%), other DoD staff (64%), national security staff in other federal agencies (59%), and policy makers in the legislative branch (42%) (see Table 5-2). Minerva researchers have provided briefings for a range of entities, including the United States Central Command, the United States Special Operations Command, the White House National Security Advisor, the National Security Agency, and the United Nations Security Council. DoD leadership and program managers reported receiving positive feedback about the usefulness of these briefings and their influence on policy decisions.

Despite these activities, however, the committee identified the need for more work to maximize opportunities for dissemination. Approximately one of three responding grantees said that opportunities to interact with national security staff and policy makers had not increased at all as a result of their participation in the Minerva program, while only about one of four said these types of opportunities had greatly increased, even with DoD staff. Opportunities for interaction with policy makers in the legislative branch were the least likely to be reported, with just 13 percent of grantees saying these opportunities had increased greatly, and 50 percent reporting that they had not increased at all.

Increased opportunities for dissemination and assistance with increasing the visibility of their work was also one of the most frequently cited changes to the Minerva program that grantees would like to see (mentioned by 14% of the grantees when asked in an open-ended format; see Appendix E, Q14). Grantees also raised related concerns when asked about challenges specific to conducting research relevant to national security (compared with research in other areas). The challenges mentioned included lack of interest in or understanding of social science among military leaders and national security stakeholders (5%), lack of adoption of findings by military leaders and national security stakeholders (5%), and lack of dissemination opportunities in general (4%).

Information gleaned from the survey of grantees and interviews with DoD staff indicates that many of the grantees disseminate their work very actively in the form of presentations, briefings, and publications in various venues beyond peer-reviewed journals. Over the years, Minerva directors and program managers have also facilitated opportunities for grantees to discuss their research with DoD staff or others in the broader national security community. However, DoD's role in systematically identifying these types of opportunities has been relatively limited to date, and DoD staff attributed this to staffing limitations.

With the new deputy director in place since 2018, several efforts to increase dissemination have been initiated, such as the redesigned website

TABLE 5-2 Grantees' Perceptions of Opportunities for Research and Dissemination as a Result of Minerva Grants (percentages)

Area of Opportunity	Greatly Increased Opportunities	Somewhat Increased Opportunities	Did Not Increase Opportunities at All	Not Applicable
Pursuing research in new directions related to the national security topics funded by the Minerva program	76	20	1	3
Expanding networks with other researchers interested in national security research	49	46	4	1
Participating in interdisciplinary and cross-disciplinary research	46	37	16	1
Providing training opportunities for students and postdoctoral scholars/fellows	53	36	5	7
Interacting with service branch staff (Air Force, Army, or Navy) interested in integrating basic research insights into their work	26	42	28	4
Interacting with other DoD staff	26	38	30	5
Interacting with national security policy staff in other federal agencies	22	37	34	7
Interacting with policy makers in the legislative branch (e.g., through congressional testimony, meetings with staff or members)	13	29	50	8

NOTES: Sample size = 76; Grantee survey Q7: "For each of the following activities, did the Minerva program greatly increase, somewhat increase, or not increase at all your opportunities?"

for the program, a new blog ("Owl in the Olive Tree") to showcase the grantees' work, and greater use of social media to distribute information about the program and its funded research. DoD is also working on compiling a comprehensive list of all grants and planning on posting this list to the DoD website (lists of grants awarded have been posted on the previous version of the website, but have not been kept up to date). These efforts, particularly the development of a comprehensive database of the grantees' work, are important because having an inventory of the research and the associated expertise is a necessary first step in being able to identify how the work can be useful for the broader national security community.

The committee believes that conducting basic research and developing human capital are complementary activities. Dissemination efforts are most valuable if they promote not only the research produced under the Minerva grants but also the expertise of the researchers. Doing so helps build a community of researchers and make available a group of scholars who can provide assistance in addressing immediate needs.

Some of the information in the database of grants (for example, topics, names, and expertise of the principal investigators [PIs]) needs to be made public to increase the usefulness of the Minerva research to others, outside of DoD. Ideally, this information would be searchable, using keywords. To implement a public-facing version of the database of grants, DoD could consider having a repository hosted by a third party, such as an academic institution. Testing this version of the database with the help of potential users as it was being developed would ensure that it would become a user-friendly resource.

RECOMMENDATION 5.2: The public-facing component of the grantee database to be developed by the Minerva program office should include detailed information about the funded projects, providing a current and historical picture of the portfolio of research that has been conducted and an inventory of the researchers' expertise. The database should be user-friendly and searchable. (See also Recommendation 3.3 in Chapter 3.)

Simultaneously with the development of the grantee database, it is essential for the Minerva staff to begin establishing both formal and informal mechanisms for interaction between grantees and DoD staff, as well as others who could learn from the research. Policy staff have expressed an interest in being able to reach out to a group of Minerva researchers with expertise on a specific topic and obtain input relatively quickly. Developing procedures to facilitate such access to the researchers would greatly increase the usefulness of the Minerva research and researchers. Possibilities could also include organizing brief, targeted sessions with research and policy staff within DoD and other agencies, policy makers in the legislative branch, policy researchers and advisors with think tanks, and others. Importantly, any procedures for interaction with Minerva researchers would need to include the handling of grantee travel funds for trips of this type. It appears that to engage in such interaction, grantees must use travel funds budgeted for this purpose as part of their projects, so it might help to clarify this point ahead of time, when grantees are developing their budgets.

> RECOMMENDATION 5.3: The Minerva program office should develop mechanisms for facilitating interaction between grantees and potential users of their research or expertise in the broader national security community.

Professional military education institutions represent an opportunity to reach additional stakeholders, particularly future leaders in the national security community. Several years ago, DoD attempted to introduce grants targeted at such institutions as part of Minerva, launching the Minerva Research for Defense Education Faculty program. This program was discontinued, however, because many of the proposals received did not meet DoD's expectations. DoD is now attempting to launch a new program—the Defense Education Civilian University Research Partnership—to award grants for basic research projects that involve collaboration between two co-PIs: one from a professional military education institution and one from a civilian research university. The Minerva program office also could consider facilitating the introduction of Minerva researchers to professional military education institutions by helping to organize seminars, elective courses, or visiting professorships.

> RECOMMENDATION 5.4: The Minerva program office should continue to explore collaborations with professional military education institutions to expose future leaders in the national security community to the program.

The main dissemination mechanism for Minerva research is the Minerva Conference, which appears to be a highly regarded event that both grantees and the broader national security community find very useful. The goal is to hold the conference annually, although no conference was held in 2017, when the program had only an interim director. While efforts have been made to encourage participation by and interaction with the policy community as part of these conferences, the 2018 event, which the committee attended, was not particularly outward-facing. Planning for the event took place at the last minute as a result of changes in the Minerva program staffing, and this may have contributed to lighter attendance than has been typical among the broader community. One might also argue that there are some benefits to keeping a conference of this type relatively small (along the lines of a "program review," which was the official title of the event) to facilitate greater interaction and more candid discussion. In that case, it might be useful to consider holding an additional conference, or perhaps lengthening the current one by an extra day, to enable an event that is more outward-facing. This outward-facing event would be focused primarily on showcasing the outcomes of the research generated by Minerva grantees, and less on academic discussion of research methods. Its agenda could also include discussions focused on future directions for the Minerva program.

RECOMMENDATION 5.5: The Minerva Conference should continue to serve as a key mechanism for outreach, dissemination, and interaction and should be held annually, on a predictable schedule.

As discussed, one of the challenges associated with the dissemination of Minerva work is that the program is intended to support basic research (referred to as 6.1 research within DoD), which, by definition, tends not to have immediate policy applications. Service branch program managers reported to the committee that they are always on the lookout for follow-on funding sources that could be a good match for the grantees they oversee, and have helped identify additional funding for some of the Minerva projects. Indeed, it appears to be relatively common for grantees to receive additional funding through the Minerva program to build on their initial work, as was the case for 38 percent of the grantees who responded to the committee's survey (see Appendix E, Q10 and Q11). Another 17 percent of the responding grantees said they had received additional funding through some other DoD funding stream, while 41 percent said they had received funding from a non-DoD source for research building on their Minerva work. Approximately one in four of those who received additional funding from another source received a grant from the National Science Foundation, another frequent source of funding for follow-up work being the PI's own academic institution.

It is unclear how much of the additional research funding obtained by grantees after a Minerva project can be described as being for applied research. Several Minerva projects appear to have produced tools and other outputs that could be well positioned to garner funding set aside for applied research (6.2 funding). There is no obvious funding stream at DoD, however, that would be a clear fit for grantees who would like to conduct applied research building on their Minerva work.

Stakeholders, including DoD staff who provided input to the committee, appear to agree that the basic research conducted under the Minerva program is valuable and should not be compromised in the interest of an increased focus on applied research. In 2005, the National Academies conducted a congressionally mandated study in response to concerns that DoD basic research funds were increasingly being used for research that did not meet the criteria of basic research. The committee that carried out that study recommended favoring "unfettered exploration" over "research related to short-term needs" for 6.1 research, and recommended further that DoD "should abandon its view of basic research as being part of a sequential or linear process of research and development . . . [and] should view basic research, applied research, and the other phases of research and development as continuing activities that occur in parallel, with numerous supporting connections among them" (National Research Council, 2005, p. 5).

As discussed, the Minerva program office has requested separate funding for 6.2 research, but the first such request did not have sufficient support within DoD. Ultimately, support for 6.2 research is an issue that goes beyond the Minerva Research Initiative.

DISCUSSION OF MINERVA'S VISION AND GOALS

The committee was asked to address whether there are ways in which the fundamentals of the vision and goals of the Minerva Research Initiative need to change to better address contemporary security needs. The vision for the Minerva program is to "support social science for a safer world" by improving "DoD's basic understanding of the social, cultural, behavioral, and political forces that shape regions of the world of strategic importance to the U.S." To accomplish its goals, the program "brings together universities, research institutions, and individual scholars and supports interdisciplinary and cross-institutional projects addressing specific topic areas determined by the Secretary of Defense."

There is clear support for Minerva's vision among those involved with the program, as well as the experts from the broader national security community who provided input to the committee. It is also clear that some challenges have been associated with implementing the program's vision, particularly with respect to balancing the characteristics of basic research with more immediate policy needs, balancing the needs of the service branches and the Office of the Secretary of Defense (OSD), balancing longer-term policy objectives and shorter-term concerns within OSD, and considering alignment with the National Defense Strategy. These challenges have manifested especially in negotiating the selection of topics and specific projects to fund. Given the recently implemented changes that shift more of the responsibility for developing topics from OSD to the service branches, DoD staff prefer to wait to see how this restructuring functions before considering further changes, an approach the committee finds reasonable, except for the specific changes recommended in this report.

The challenges associated with reconciling the goals of basic research and policy relevance were also evident in comments made to the committee by representatives of the broader national security community who were asked about their views on the program's vision. They made several suggestions for expanding outreach to obtain broader input on topics to fund. An example was to establish an advisory board for the Minerva program, possibly including chief scientists from each of the commands. Another suggestion was to survey a broader community of researchers and policy makers to request input on research priorities—perhaps similar to the decadal surveys that have been conducted by the National Academies in several fields (see, for example, National Academies of Sciences, Engineering, and Medicine, 2019a). At the same time, these experts encouraged enough consistency in the topics funded from year to year to allow for a body of knowledge to develop.

The input received by the committee from all sources underscored continued support for the key aspects of the original vision of the Minerva program, including its interdisciplinary nature, as well as the importance of keeping the work transparent and unclassified. Overall, the input received by the committee did not reveal a need for major changes in the types of research that are funded or the size or duration of grants.

At the same time, DoD needs to carefully consider the program's priorities with respect to addressing immediate versus longer-term research needs, serving DoD-wide versus service branch interests, and emphasizing scientific merit versus policy relevance. DoD also needs to consider the implications of these priorities for the program's organizational structure and other features of its implementation. Having these priorities defined more clearly would reduce some of the friction that currently characterizes the relationships among the program's internal stakeholders, and could potentially address some of the concerns that led to the Army's decision to withdraw from the program.

> RECOMMENDATION 5.6: The Minerva program office should specify its priorities for the Minerva Research Initiative, and, as needed, refine the program's approach to topic selection and grant award to reflect these priorities.

INCREASING SOCIAL SCIENTISTS' ENGAGEMENT WITH THE PROGRAM

The committee found no evidence to suggest serious problems with the engagement of social scientists or, in particular, early-career scholars with the Minerva program. Nonetheless, there is room for improvement in this area, particularly with regard to promoting broader awareness of the program across the social science research community and more active roles for early-career researchers.

DoD staff reported that the Minerva grants are competitive and that strong proposals are routinely turned down. It is also evident, however, that some potential stakeholders have never heard of the program. Of the 88 respondents who completed the survey on behalf of university offices of sponsored research, 40 percent said they were "not familiar at all" with the Minerva program, and an additional 34 percent said they were "not too familiar" (see Appendix F, Q1). The committee had no ideal way of identifying the most suitable respondents for the survey of administrators of sponsored research in every case, and this may have been a limitation on the information obtained. Nonetheless, 90 percent of the respondents said they either personally had experience working with other (non-Minerva) grants from the DoD service branches or were aware of their colleagues working with such grants. Thus, despite widespread familiarity with DoD grants generally, university administrators of sponsored research have only limited familiarity with Minerva grants.

Researchers tend to learn about the Minerva program by word of mouth. Table 5-3, based on responses from the grantee survey, shows the percentage of respondents who had heard about the Minerva program from various sources. The most frequently cited source, by far, was "a colleague," suggesting possible opportunities for developing new or improving existing outreach efforts to take a more systematic approach.

Among the grants awarded to date, 87 have been at doctoral universities with the highest levels of research activity, 10 at doctoral universities with higher levels of research activity, and 3 at doctoral universities with moderate levels of research activity, as categorized by the Carnegie

TABLE 5-3 Grantees' Sources of Information about Minerva Grants (percentages)

Source	Yes
University research office	29
Department of Defense (DoD) website	37
National Science Foundation	22
A conference	34
A colleague	79
Mailing list	21
Other—please specify	11

NOTES: Sample size = 76; Grantee survey Q1: "Prior to applying for a Minerva grant, did you learn about the Minerva grant program in any of the following ways?"

Classification of Institutions of Higher Education (see Appendix L). One grant was at an institution that does not have a Carnegie code, and 8 grants have been awarded to researchers at universities abroad. Among 64 institutions receiving Minerva grants, 26 were awarded more than one grant (this number includes institutions where some PIs have received more than one grant, but also institutions that have had two or more faculty with different Minerva grants).

With respect to the Minerva program's reach across the social sciences, the grants attract researchers from many different disciplines. Approximately half of the grants have been awarded to PIs whose highest degree is in a subfield of political science, broadly defined. Psychology and economics, as well as mathematics and computer science, are also well represented, with around 10 percent of the grants awarded each. In addition, grants have been awarded to PIs with backgrounds in other social science fields, such as sociology, anthropology, demography, and criminology, as well as such fields as law, engineering, and physics. Many projects have involved cross-disciplinary collaborations.

Representatives of social science associations reported to the committee that in some fields, there is awareness of the Minerva program mainly among researchers focused on a specific subfield (for example, those working on issues related to intergroup conflict within the broader field of psychology). Others observed that early-career academics may be less aware of the program than more established researchers. This is the case particularly among anthropologists because the American Anthropological Association's high-profile involvement in debates about the program when it was first launched attracted a great deal of attention within that field. However, this also appears to be the case among political scientists, even though there is much more overlap among the areas of specialization of political scientists and the Minerva topics funded relative to the field of anthropology, and several prominent political scientists have been PIs on Minerva grants.

Representatives of social science associations who met with the committee noted that the DoD website contained very little information about the Minerva program. This was due in part to the transition to a new website during the course of the committee's evaluation. Among the specific suggestions made regarding the types of information that could make the website more useful to researchers, particularly those not yet familiar with the program, were examples of the work conducted by researchers from various disciplines, discussion of how the research could be used to reduce conflict or avoid wars (in contrast with the language of the 2018 National Defense Strategy to "build a more lethal force"), and a description of the potentially positive impact of the research on the populations studied. The ongoing efforts to improve the Minerva website could address these suggestions.

As the staffing in the Minerva program office stabilizes, another area in which increased efforts by program staff could enhance the engagement of social scientists in the Minerva program is participation in the conferences of professional associations. For example, Minerva staff could disseminate information about the program at conferences by participating as exhibitors. A symposium at an American Association for the Advancement of Science meeting could also be considered.

Occasionally, the Minerva grant announcements have been released later than the typical grant cycle, primarily as a result of the program staffing challenges discussed previously in this report. A short turnaround time can have the unintended consequence of increasing the ratio of repeat applications (including from existing grantees) to new applications. Grant announcements issued on a predictable schedule could therefore increase the diversity of the applicant pool.

Similar to planning for outreach and dissemination (see Recommendation 5.1), efforts to inform a broader community about the Minerva program and build engagement need to be based on a carefully developed plan that identifies strategic objectives and how they can be achieved. As discussed earlier, it is notable that about three-quarters of the administrators of sponsored research said they were not familiar at all or not too familiar with the Minerva program. Discussions with stakeholders are needed to inform the development of the plan for broadening engagement with the program. Having a staff member specifically focused on outreach activities could be particularly helpful.

RECOMMENDATION 5.7: The Minerva program office should develop and implement a plan for further broadening engagement with the Minerva Research Initiative based on strategically identified objectives with respect to the target groups of researchers to engage and systematic steps for how to reach and engage them.

Engaging early-career researchers is particularly important to support the continued success of the program and cultivate the next generation of academics with interest in conducting social science research relevant to national security. One productive way of engaging these scholars is to include students and postdoctoral fellows on the Minerva project teams, an approach that is encouraged by DoD. When PIs were asked about whether their Minerva grants provided training opportunities for students and postdoctoral scholars/fellows, 53 percent said these opportunities had been greatly increased by the Minerva projects, and 36 percent said they had been somewhat increased. Among those who provided a response about the number of students or fellows actively involved in their Minerva grant for at least one academic quarter or semester, the median number of undergraduate students was three, of graduate students was four, and of postdoctoral fellows was one, with quite a bit of variation across projects. Larger projects can likely include students and postdocs more easily.

As an additional opportunity for early-career scholars, DoD recently launched a collaboration with the United States Institute of Peace (USIP). The Minerva Research Initiative's Peace and Security fellowships are awarded to graduate students working on research related to their dissertation. Priority topics for this funding are determined jointly by DoD and USIP. During the most recent round of funding, more than 220 applications were received, and 12 fellowships were awarded.

DoD already receives applications for the Minerva grants from a mix of early-career and more senior researchers, but to further bolster interest among the next generation of researchers, has discussed the possibility of tailoring smaller awards for early-career academics. Such awards could potentially reduce the time investment required of grantees to perform administrative tasks associated with larger, more complex projects. In addition, smaller grants placing less emphasis on interdisciplinary collaboration might be more appealing to early-career academics, who are rewarded more substantially for publications in their own discipline. On the other hand, larger grants can enable researchers to reduce their teaching load, which may be particularly important to early-career researchers.

Some DoD staff expressed the view that one barrier to participation by early-career researchers might be greater caution about accepting DoD funding and its perceived implications for their career. When grantees were asked about challenges associated with conducting (unclassified) research relevant to national security, only 12 percent mentioned criticism from academic colleagues due to DoD funding, which suggests that these types of concerns are not pervasive. Nevertheless, they may influence the decisions of early-career scholars about what research to undertake. Among administrators of sponsored programs, 11 percent agreed with the statement that "most people at my institution have unfavorable views of conducting national security research in general," and the numbers were similar when they were asked specifically about the views of social science faculty (although most said they did not know).

The annual Minerva Conference provides an important venue for outreach, and it can be particularly productive for outreach focused specifically on early-career academics, who sometimes have less visibility and engagement at conferences relative to the senior researchers on their teams. The Minerva Conference could include informational sessions or other such activities (for example, meetings with senior DoD leaders) focused on early-career researchers. In addition, the Minerva program office could facilitate more active roles for these researchers in presenting their work at the conference, perhaps through specifically targeted or structured sessions.

RECOMMENDATION 5.8: The Minerva program office should consider organizing activities for early-career researchers at the Minerva Conference to provide them with information about substantive topics in national security, as well as research opportunities and guidance about how to take advantage of those opportunities.

RECOMMENDATION 5.9: The Minerva program office should encourage more active roles for early-career researchers on existing Minerva project teams in presenting the research at the Minerva Conference.

DEVELOPING BENCHMARKS FOR CONTINUOUS MONITORING AND EVALUATION

As the Minerva program approaches its tenth year, it will be important to develop benchmarks for ongoing monitoring and evaluation of the program, based on the priorities identified by DoD staff. In specifying these benchmarks, however, the Minerva program office needs to ensure that striving to reach one benchmark does not create an unanticipated incentive that might compromise achieving other goals of the program. For example, the benchmarks should not discourage the funding of high-risk projects if they have the potential for high reward.

RECOMMENDATION 5.10: The Minerva program office should develop specific benchmarks for use in continuously monitoring and evaluating the Minerva Research Initiative's accomplishments and challenges going forward. These benchmarks should be measured and assessed on a regular basis, possibly annually or biennially.

Given increasing emphasis on open-science practices and other efforts to improve reproducibility and replicability in research (National Academies of Sciences, Engineering, and Medicine, 2019b), it will also be important for the Minerva program office to monitor how research standards evolve in the context of the disciplines relevant to the Minerva program and to be at the forefront of implementing transparency and other requirements that encourage best practices, as they become established.

References

Agarwal, A., Durairajanayagam, D., Tatagari, S., Esteves, S.C., Harlev, A., Henkel, R., Roychoudhury, S., Homa, S., Puchalt, N.G., Ramasamy, R., Majzoub, A., Ly, K.D., Tvrda, E., Assidi, M., Kesari, K., Sharma, R., Banihani, S., Ko, E., Abu-Elmagd, M., Gosalvez, J., and Bashiri, A. (2016). Bibliometrics: Tracking research impact by selecting the appropriate metrics. *Asian Journal of Andrology, 18*(2), 296–309. doi:10.4103/1008-682X.171582.

Bornmann, L., and Marx, W. (2013). How good is research really?: Measuring the citation impact of publications with percentiles increases correct assessments and fair comparisons. *EMBO Reports, 14*(3), 226–230. doi:10.1038/embor.2013.9.

Department of Defense. (2008). *Secretary of Defense Speech*. Available: http://archive.defense.gov/Speeches/Speech.aspx?SpeechID=1228.

Department of Defense. (2017). *Financial Management Regulation*. DoD 7000.14-R. Available: https://comptroller.defense.gov/portals/45/documents/fmr/current/02b/02b_05.pdf.

Department of Defense Washington Headquarters Services/Acquisition Directorate. (2018). *Minerva Research Initiative*. FOA #WHS-AD-FOA-18. Available: https://www.grants.gov/web/grants/search-grants.html?keywords=whs-ad-foa-18 (June 2019).

deRijke, S., Wouters, P.F., Rushforth, A.D., Franssen, T.P., and Hammarfelt, B. (2015). Evaluation practices and effects of indicator use—a literature review. *Research Evaluation, 25*(2), 161–169.

Desch, M. (2019). *Cult of the Irrelevant: The Waning Influence of Social Science on National Security*. Princeton, NJ: Princeton University Press.

González-Pereira, B., Guerrero-Bote, V.P., and Moya-Anegón, F. (2010). A new approach to the metric of journals' scientific prestige: The SJR indicator. *Journal of Informetrics, 4*(3), 379–391. doi:10.1016/j.joi.2010.03.002.

Hicks, D., and Melkers, J. (2013). Bibliometrics as a tool for research evaluation. In A. Link and N. Vornatas (Eds.), *Handbook on the Theory and Practice of Program Evaluation* (pp. 323–349). Cheltenham, UK: Edward Elgar Publishing.

Hicks, D., and Wouters, P. (2015). The Leiden Manifesto for research metrics. *Nature, 520*(23), 429–431.

Indiana University Center for Postsecondary Research. (2016). *Carnegie Classifications 2015 Public Data File.* Available: http://carnegieclassifications.iu.edu/downloads/CCIHE2015-PublicDataFile.xlsx.

James, C., Colledge, L., Meester, W., Azoulay, N., and Plume. (2018). *CiteScore Metrics: Creating Journal Metrics from the Scopus Citation Index.* Available: https://arxiv.org/ftp/arxiv/papers/1812/1812.06871.pdf.

Low, S.M. (2008). *Letter to the Honorable Jim Nussle, Office of Management and Budget, May 28.* Available: http://s3.amazonaws.com/rdcms-aaa/files/production/public/FileDownloads/pdfs/issues/policy-advocacy/upload/Minerva-Letter.pdf.

Minerva Research Initiative. (n.d.). *About Minerva.* Available: https://minerva.defense.gov/About.

Moed, H.F. (2017). *Applied Evaluative Informatics.* Switzerland: Springer International Publishing.

Montgomery, D. (2019, January). *Minerva and Social Science.* OUSD-R&E Briefing. Presentation slides provided to the committee.

Nair, B. (2018, January 16). *Minerva Research Initiative Program Review Kick-Off.* Presentation prepared for the Committee to Assess the Minerva Research Initiative and the Contribution of Social Science to Addressing Security Concerns, Washington, DC.

National Academies of Sciences, Engineering, and Medicine. (2019a). *A Decadal Survey of the Social and Behavioral Sciences: A Research Agenda for Advancing Intelligence Analysis.* Washington, DC: The National Academies Press. doi:10.17226/25335.

National Academies of Sciences, Engineering, and Medicine (2019b). *Reproducibility and Replicability in Science.* Washington, DC: The National Academies Press. https://doi.org/10.17226/25303.

National Research Council. (2005). *Assessment of Department of Defense Basic Research.* Committee on Department of Defense Basic Research, Division on Engineering and Physical Sciences. Washington, DC: The National Academies Press. doi:10.17226/11177.

National Science Foundation. (2008). *Social and Behavioral Dimensions of National Security, Conflict, and Cooperation (NSCC).* Program Solicitation NSF 08-594. Available: https://www.nsf.gov/pubs/2008/nsf08594/nsf08594.htm.

National Science Foundation. (2014). *The National Science Foundation Proposal and Award Policies and Procedures Guide.* NSF 15-1. Available: https://www.nsf.gov/pubs/policydocs/pappguide/nsf15001/nsf15_1.pdf.

National Science Foundation and Department of Defense. (2008). *Memorandum of Understanding.* Document provided by DoD to the committee.

Scopus. (2019a). *FAQs for the Content Selection Process.* Available: https://www.elsevier.com/solutions/scopus/how-scopus-works/content/content-policy-and-selection.

Scopus. (2019b). *How Are Article Metrics Used in Scopus? Metric and Definition: Field Weighted Citation Impact and Citation Benchmarking.* Available: https://service.elsevier.com/app/answers/detail/a_id/12031/supporthub/scopus.

Scopus. (2019c). *How Are CiteScore Metrics Used in Scopus? What Are the Other CiteScore Metrics? CiteScore Percentiles.* Available: https://service.elsevier.com/app/answers/detail/a_id/14880/supporthub/scopus.

Scopus. (2019d). *How Are CiteScore Metrics Used in Scopus? What Is the CiteScore Methodology?* Available: https://service.elsevier.com/app/answers/detail/a_id/14880/supporthub/scopus.

Scopus. (2019e). *How Is SJR (SCImago Journal Rank) Used in Scopus?* Available: https://service.elsevier.com/app/answers/detail/a_id/14883/supporthub/scopus/related/1.

Scopus. (2019f). *What Is Peer Review?* Available: https://www.elsevier.com/en-gb/reviewers/what-is-peer-review.

REFERENCES

Scopus. (2019g). *What Is the Complete List of Scopus Subject Areas and All Science Journal Classification Codes (ASJC)?* Available: https://service.elsevier.com/app/answers/detail/a_id/15181/supporthub/scopus.

Siler, K., Lee, K., and Bero, L. (2015). Measuring the effectiveness of scientific gatekeeping. *Proceedings of the National Academy of Sciences of the United States of America, 12*(2), 360–365. doi:10.1073/pnas.1418218112.

Stokes, D.E. (1997). *Pasteur's Quadrant: Basic Science and Technological Innovation.* Washington, DC: The Brookings Institution.

Sugimoto, C.R., and Lariviere, V. (2018). *Measuring Research: What Everyone Needs to Know.* New York: Oxford University Press.

Testa, J. (2017, September). The selection process for the book citation index in Web of Science. *Clarivate Analytics.* Available: https://clarivate.com/essays/selection-process-book-citation-index-web-science.

Ulrich's Web. (n.d.). *Frequently Asked Questions, About the Ulrich's Knowledgebase, What Is a Refereed Serial?* Available: http://www.ulrichsweb.com/ulrichsweb/faqs.asp.

Web of Science. (2019). *Conference Proceedings Selection Process.* Available: https://clarivate.com/essays/web-science-conference-proceedings-selection-process.

Appendix A

Federal Obligations for Basic Research

TABLE A-1 2017 Preliminary Federal Obligations for Basic Research, by Agency and Field of Science and Engineering (dollars in thousands)

Agency	Total	Computer Sciences and Mathematics	Engineering	Environmental Sciences	Life Sciences	Physical Sciences	Psychology	Social Sciences	Other Sciences Not Elsewhere Classified
All Agencies	32,331,733	1,995,441	3,631,804	2,660,886	15,864,610	4,671,434	1,000,750	392,835	2,113,973
Department of Agriculture	980,061	874	23,391	5,458	857,101	49,810	0	43,427	0
Agricultural Research Service	570,826	742	5,137	2,512	524,418	36,647	0	1,370	0
Animal and Plant Health Inspection Service	18,856	0	0	0	18,856	0	0	0	0
Foreign Agricultural Service	38	0	0	0	38	0	0	0	0
Forest Service	82,708	132	3,325	1,605	63,865	3,333	0	10,449	0
National Institute of Food and Agriculture	307,633	0	14,929	1,342	249,924	9,830	0	31,608	0
Department of Commerce	248,368	27,499	28,871	0	9,613	172,008	0	0	10,377
National Institute of Standards and Technology	248,368	27,499	28,871	0	9,613	172,008	0	0	10,377

Department of Defense	2,313,315	483,784	546,867	101,542	239,903	343,692	32,023	40,206	525,298
Defense Advanced Research Projects Agency	434,819	197,438	63,385	0	90,154	18,104	0	0	65,739
Department of the Air Force	515,928	57,023	192,037	14,578	31,573	158,709	1,746	29	60,233
Department of the Army	505,854	160,683	161,968	21,436	60,264	61,003	13,353	13,077	14,071
Department of the Navy	634,411	37,920	85,333	62,534	22,163	62,562	9,922	4,275	349,701
Other defense agencies	222,305	30,720	44,144	2,994	35,751	43,314	7,003	22,825	35,554
Department of Education	42,095	0	0	0	0	0	0	2,906	39,189
Department of Energy	4,553,981	475,751	968,246	297,568	410,578	1,908,725	0	0	493,113
Bonneville Power Administration	5,469	1,669	3,800	0	0	0	0	0	0
Electricity Delivery and Energy Reliability	6,800	0	6,800	0	0	0	0	0	0
Fossil Energy	6	0	0	0	0	6	0	0	0
National Nuclear Security Administration	88,793	6,082	1,250	6,804	435	74,201	0	0	21
Nuclear Nonproliferation	88,793	6,082	1,250	6,804	435	74,201	0	0	21
Nuclear Energy	23,859	0	23,859	0	0	0	0	0	0
Office of Science	4,429,054	468,000	932,537	290,764	410,143	1,834,518	0	0	493,092

continued

TABLE A-1 Continued

Agency	Total	Computer Sciences and Mathematics	Engineering	Environmental Sciences	Life Sciences	Physical Sciences	Psychology	Social Sciences	Other Sciences Not Elsewhere Classified
Department of Health and Human Services	15,865,744	68,929	831,489	190,051	13,252,691	55,093	915,090	62,810	489,592
Centers for Disease Control and Prevention	72,220	0	0	33,710	20,493	0	1,007	227	16,782
Health Resources and Services Administration	2,524	0	0	0	2,524	0	0	0	0
National Institutes of Health	15,791,000	68,929	831,489	156,341	13,229,674	55,093	914,083	62,583	472,809
Department of Homeland Security	11,566	0	0	0	0	0	0	0	11,566
Domestic Nuclear Detection Office	11,566	0	0	0	0	0	0	0	11,566
Department of the Interior	54,340	0	0	31,217	13,682	8,954	0	488	0
U.S. Geological Survey	54,340	0	0	31,217	13,682	8,954	0	488	0
Department of Justice	11,977	0	0	0	0	0	0	11,977	0
Office of Justice Programs	11,977	0	0	0	0	0	0	11,977	0
Department of the Treasury	1,899	0	0	0	0	1,899	0	0	0
Bureau of Engraving and Printing	1,899	0	0	0	0	1,899	0	0	0

Department of Veterans Affairs	209,009	0	6,270	0	188,108	0	14,631	0
National Aeronautics and Space Administration	2,926,010	29,030	541,320	831,014	129,808	1,151,730	5,152	900	237,056
National Science Foundation	4,900,000	909,576	685,349	1,194,145	667,650	918,224	33,854	186,174	305,028
Nuclear Regulatory Commission	1,435	0	0	0	0	0	0	0	1,435
Smithsonian Institution	211,933	0	0	9,891	95,475	61,299	0	43,948	1,320

NOTES: Because of rounding, detail may not add to total. Only those agencies and subdivisions that had obligations in fields represented by this table appear in the table.

SOURCE: National Science Foundation, National Center for Science and Engineering Statistics, Survey of Federal Funds for Research and Development, FYs 2016–17. Available: https://ncsesdata.nsf.gov/fedfunds/2016/html/ffs2016_dst_031.html.

TABLE A-2 2016 Federal Obligations for Basic Research Performed at Universities and Colleges in Social Sciences, by Selected Agency and Detailed Field (dollars in thousands)

Agency	Total	Anthropology	Economics	Political Science	Sociology	Other Social Sciences
All Agencies Surveyed by NSF	254,853	21,921	33,925	13,456	12,822	172,729
Departments						
Department of Agriculture	22,919	0	16,238	0	6,456	225
Agricultural Research Service	100	0	100	0	0	0
Forest Service	404	0	59	0	120	225
National Institute of Food and Agriculture	22,416	0	16,080	0	6,335	0
Department of Defense	28,174	3,638	0	4,518	1,365	18,653
Department of the Army	2,920	0	0	0	0	2,920
Department of the Navy	3,529	3,529	0	0	0	0
Other defense agencies	21,725	109	0	4,518	1,365	15,733
Department of Health and Human Services	43,381	0	0	0	0	43,381
Centers for Disease Control and Prevention	285	0	0	0	0	285
National Institutes of Health	43,096	0	0	0	0	43,096
Other agencies						
National Aeronautics and Space Administration	187	0	0	0	68	119
National Science Foundation	160,192	18,283	17,687	8,937	4,934	110,352

NOTES: Because of rounding, detail may not add to total. Seven agencies are required to report data for this section of the survey: the Departments of Agriculture, Defense, Energy, Health and Human Services, and Homeland Security; the National Aeronautics and Space Administration; and the National Science Foundation. Basic research obligations of these seven agencies represented greater than 99% of total federal basic research obligations to universities and colleges in FY 2016. Only those agencies and subdivisions that had obligations in fields represented by this table appear in the table.
SOURCE: National Science Foundation, National Center for Science and Engineering Statistics, Survey of Federal Funds for Research and Development, FYs 2016–17. Available: https://ncsesdata.nsf.gov/fedfunds/2016/html/ffs2016_dst_075.html.

Appendix B

Minerva Research Topics in Grant Announcements Issued between 2008 and 2018

Information about the research topics funded by the Minerva program was compiled from the grant announcements listed below. The research topics are described in further detail in their respective grant announcements.

2008 Broad Agency Announcement issued by DoD Army Research Office (W911NF-08-R-0007)
Available at: https://www.arl.army.mil/www/default.cfm?page=362

1. Chinese Military and Technology Research and Archive Programs
2. Studies of the Strategic Impact of Religious and Cultural Changes within the Islamic World
3. Iraqi Perspective Project
4. Studies of Terrorist Organizations and Ideologies
5. New Approaches to Understanding Dimensions of National Security, Conflict, and Cooperation

2008 Program Solicitation issued for NSF-DoD Partnership by National Science Foundation–Social and Behavioral Dimensions of National Security, Conflict, and Cooperation (NSCC) (NSF 08-594)
Available at: https://www.nsf.gov/pubs/2008/nsf08594/nsf08594.pdf

1. New Approaches to Understanding Dimensions of National Security, Conflict, and Cooperation
2. Studies of Terrorist Organization and Ideologies
3. Studies of Political, Cultural, and Social Dynamics Under Authoritarian Regimes

2011 Broad Agency Announcement issued by DoD Army Research Office (W911NF-11-R-0011)
Available at: https://www.arl.army.mil/www/default.cfm?page=362

1. Strategic Impact of Religious and Cultural Changes
2. Terrorism and Terrorist Ideologies
3. Science, Technology and Military Transformations in China and Developing States
4. National Security Implications of Energy and Environmental Stress
5. New Theories of Cross-Domain Deterrence
6. Regime and Social Dynamics in Failed, Failing, and Fragile Authoritarian States
7. New Approaches to Understanding Dimensions of National Security, Conflict, and Cooperation

2012 Broad Agency Announcement issued by DoD Office of Naval Research (ONR BAA 12-016)
Available at: https://www.onr.navy.mil/work-with-us/funding-opportunities/announcements

1. Belief Formation and Movements for Change
   a) Belief formation and influence
   b) Group identities and cultural norms
   c) Movements for change
   d) Collaboration and competition between violent groups

2. Models of Societal Resilience and Change
   a) Economic factors
   b) Energy, environment, and resource factors
   c) Other factors impacting societal stability and change

3. Theories of Power and Deterrence
   a) The role of the state in a globalized world
   b) Norms and governance
   c) Beyond conventional deterrence
   d) Emerging topics in power and deterrence

APPENDIX B

2013 Broad Agency Announcement issued by DoD Office of Naval Research (ONR BAA 13-024)

Available at: https://www.onr.navy.mil/work-with-us/funding-opportunities/announcements

1. Belief Propagation and Movements for Change
   a) Belief formation and influence
   b) Group identity, cultural norms, and security
   c) Mobilization for change
   d) The structural dynamics of disruptive organizations

2. Models of Societal Resilience and Change
   a) Economic contributors to stability
   b) Governance contributors to stability
   c) Energy, environment, and resource contributors to stability
   d) Additional factors impacting societal resilience and change

3. Theories of Power and Escalation
   a) The changing role of the state in a globalized world
   b) Beyond conventional deterrence

4. Emerging Topics in Conflict and Security
   a) Quantification and metrics
   b) Additional topics

2014 Broad Agency Announcement issued by DoD Office of Naval Research (ONR BAA 14-013)

Available at: https://www.onr.navy.mil/work-with-us/funding-opportunities/announcements

1. Identity, Influence, and Mobilization
   a) Culture, identity, and security
   b) Belief formation and influence
   c) Mobilization for change

2. Contributors to Societal Resilience and Change
   a) Governance and rule of law
   b) Resources, economics, and globalization
   c) Additional factors impacting societal resilience and change

3. Power and Deterrence
   a) Power projection and diffusion
   b) Beyond conventional deterrence

4. Innovations in National Security, Conflict, and Cooperation
   a) Analytical methods and metrics for security research
   b) Emerging topics in conflict and security

2016 Funding Opportunity Announcement issued by DoD Washington Headquarters Services/Acquisition Directorate (FOA #WHS-AD-FOA-16-01)
Available at: https://www.grants.gov/web/grants/search-grants.html

1. Identity, Influence, and Mobilization
   a) Culture, identity, and security
   b) Influence and mobilization for change

2. Contributors to Societal Resilience and Change
   a) Governance and rule of law
   b) Migration and urbanization
   c) Populations and demographics
   d) Environment and natural resources
   e) Economics

3. Power and Deterrence
   a) Global order
   b) Power projection and diffusion
   c) Beyond conventional deterrence
   d) Area studies

4. Analytic Methods and Metrics for Security Research

5. Innovations in National Security, Conflict, and Cooperation

2017 Funding Opportunity Announcement issued by DoD Washington Headquarters Services/Acquisition Directorate (FOA #WHS-AD-FOA-17-01)
Available at: https://www.grants.gov/web/grants/search-grants.html

General Interest Area: Sociality, Security, & Interconnectivity
Special Interest Area 1: Understanding the Social Impact of Autonomy
Special Interest Area 2: Societal Resilience & Sociopolitical (In)stability
Special Interest Area 3: Power & Deterrence for Shaping Operations
Special Interest Area 4: Military Cyber Defense

2018 Funding Opportunity Announcement issued by DoD Washington Headquarters Services/Acquisition Directorate (FOA #WHS-AD-FOA-18)
Available at: https://www.grants.gov/web/grants/search-grants.html

- Topic 1: Sociopolitical (In)Stability, Resilience, and Recovery
- Topic 2: Economic Interdependence and Security
- Topic 3: Alliances and Burden Sharing
- Topic 4: Fundamental Dynamics of Scientific Discovery
- Topic 5: Adversarial Information Campaigns
- Topic 6: Automated Cyber Vulnerability Analysis
- Topic 7: Power, Deterrence, Influence, and Escalation Management for Shaping Operations
- Topic 8: Security Risks in Ungoverned & Semi-Governed Spaces

Appendix C

List of Minerva Grant Awards Between 2009–2017

At the time when the committee completed its review, DoD was in the process of posting brief descriptions of funded projects to the Minerva Research Initiative website. Further information about some of the studies was available at: https://minerva.defense.gov/Research/Funded-Projects/.

TABLE C-1 List of Minerva Grant Awards between 2009 and 2017

Grant Title	Year of Grant	Principal Investigator	Principal Investigator's Affiliation (at the time of the National Academies study)
Emotion and Intergroup Relations	2009	David Matsumoto	San Francisco State University
Terrorism, Governance, and Development	2009	Jacob Shapiro	Princeton University
Iraq's Wars with the US from the Iraqi Perspective: State Security, Weapons of Mass Destruction, Civil-Military Relations, Ethnic Conflict and Political Communication in Baathist Iraq	2009	Leonard Spector	Middlebury Institute of International Studies
Finding Allies for the War of Words: Mapping the Diffusion and Influence of Counter-Radical Muslim Discourse	2009	Mark Woodward	Arizona State University
Explorations in Cyber International Relations	2009	Nazli Choucri	Massachusetts Institute of Technology
Climate Change and African Political Stability	2009	Robert Chesney	University of Texas, Austin
The Evolving Relationship Between Technology and National Security in China: Innovation, Defense Transformation, and China's Place in the Global Technology Order	2009	Tai Ming Cheung	University of California, San Diego
How Politics Inside Dictatorships Affects Regime Stability and International Conflict	2010	Barbara Geddes	University of California, Los Angeles
Behavioral Insights into National Security Issues	2010	Catherine Eckel	Texas A&M University
Experimental Analysis of Alternative Models of Conflict Bargaining	2010	Charles Holt	University of Virginia
People, Power, and Conflict in the Eurasian Migration System	2010	Cynthia Buckley	University of Illinois
Political Economy of Terrorism and Insurgency (Workshop)	2010	Eli Berman	University of California, San Diego
Engaging Intensely Adversarial States: The Strategic Limits and Potential of Public Diplomacy in U.S. National Security Policy	2010	Geoffrey Wiseman	Australian National University

Title	Year	PI	Institution
Deciphering Civil Conflict in the Middle East	2010	J. Craig Jenkins	Ohio State University
Avoiding Water Wars: Environmental Security Through River Treaty Institutionalization	2010	Jaroslav Tir	University of Colorado, Boulder
Modeling Discourse and Social Dynamics in Authoritarian Regimes	2010	Jeff Hancock	Stanford University
Predicting the Nature of Conflict - An Evolutionary Analysis of the Tactical Choice	2010	Laura Razzolini	Virginia Commonwealth University
Mapping Terrorist Organizations	2010	Martha Crenshaw	Stanford University
Status, Manipulating Group Threats, and Conflict Within and Between Groups	2010	Patrick Barclay	University of Guelph
Substantive Expertise, Strategic Analysis and Behavioral Foundations of Terrorism (Workshop)	2010	Rachel Croson	University of Texas, Arlington
Visualizing Agent Based Political Simulations	2010	Remco Chang	Tufts University
Fighting and Bargaining over Political Power in Weak States	2010	Robert Powell	University of California, Berkeley
New Armies from Old: Merging Competing Military Forces after Civil Wars (Workshop)	2010	Roy Licklider	Rutgers University
Terror, Conflict Processes, Organizations, and Ideologies: Completing the Picture	2010	Stephen Shellman	College of William and Mary
Strategies of Violence, Tools of Peace, and Changes in War Termination	2010	Virginia Fortna	Columbia University
Strategy and the Network Society	2011	David Betz	King's College, London
Motivation, Ideology, and the Social Process in Radicalization and Deradicalization	2012	Arie Kruglanski	University of Maryland
Brazil as a Major Power: The Impact of its Military-Scientific-Industrial Complex on its Foreign and Defense Policy	2012	David Mares	University of California, San Diego
Quantifying Structural Transformation in China	2012	David Meyer	University of California, San Diego
China's Emerging Capabilities in Energy Technology Innovation and Development	2012	Edward Steinfeld	Brown University

continued

TABLE C-1 Continued

Grant Title	Year of Grant	Principal Investigator	Principal Investigator's Affiliation (at the time of the National Academies study)
Identifying and Countering Early Risk Factors for Violent Extremism Among Somali Refugee Communities Resettled in North America	2012	Heidi Ellis	Boston Children's Hospital/Harvard Medical School
Autocratic Stability During Regime Crises	2012	Joseph Wright	Pennsylvania State University
Institutional Reform, Social Change, and Stability in Sahelian Africa	2012	Leonardo Villalón	University of Florida
A Global Value Chain Analysis of Food Security and Food Staples for Major Energy-Exporting Nations in the Middle East and North Africa	2012	Lincoln Pratson	Duke University
Energy and Environmental Drivers of Stress and Conflict in Multi-Scale Models of Human Social Behavior	2012	Luis Bettencourt	University of Chicago
Terrorist Alliances: Causes, Dynamics, and Consequences; (Follow-on Grant in 2015 Titled: "Assessing Cooperation and Conflict among Militant Organizations")	2012	Philip Potter	University of Virginia
Strategic Response to Energy-related Security Threats	2012	Saleem Ali	University of Queensland
Political Reach, State Fragility, and the Incidence of Maritime Piracy: Explaining Piracy and Pirate Organization, 1993–2012; Follow-on Grant in 2015 titled: "Crime in Civil Conflict"	2013	Brandon Prins	University of Tennessee, Knoxville
Forecasting Civil Conflict Under Different Climate Change Scenarios	2013	Elisabeth Gilmore	University of Maryland
Deterring Complex Threats: The Effects of Asymmetry, Interdependence, and Multi-polarity on International Strategy	2013	Erik Gartzke	University of California, San Diego
METANORM: A Multidisciplinary Approach to the Analysis and Evaluation of Norms and Models of Governance for Cyberspace	2013	Howard Shrobe	Massachusetts Institute of Technology, CSAIL

Title	Year	PI	Institution
Natural Resources and Armed Conflict	2013	James Walsh	University of North Carolina, Charlotte
Dynamics of Sacred Values and Social Responsibilities in Governance and Conflict Management: The Interplay between Leaders, Devoted Actor Networks, General Populations, and Time	2013	Jeremy Ginges	The New School for Social Research
The Human Geography of Resilience and Change: Land Rights and Political Stability in Latin American Indigenous Societies	2013	Jerome Dobson	University of Kansas
Multi-Source Assessment of State Stability	2013	Kathleen Carley	Carnegie Mellon University
Who Does Not Become a Terrorist, and Why? Towards an Empirically Grounded Understanding of Individual Motivation in Terrorism	2013	Maria Rasmussen	Naval Postgraduate School
Neural Bases of Persuasion and Social Influence in the U.S. and the Middle East	2013	Matthew Lieberman	University of California, Los Angeles
The Strength of Social Norms Across Cultures: Implications for Intercultural Conflict and Cooperation	2013	Michele Gelfand	University of Maryland
Public Service Provision as Peace-building: How do Autonomous Efforts Compare to Internationally Aided Interventions?	2013	Naazneen Barma	Naval Postgraduate School
Moral Schemas, Cultural Conflict, and Socio-Political Action	2013	Steven Hitlin	University of Iowa
Homeownership and Societal Stability: Assessing Causal Effects in Central Eurasia	2013	Ted Gerber	University of Wisconsin, Madison
Deterrence with Proxies	2014	Eli Berman	University of California, San Diego
Does Current Investment Predict Future Violence: Lessons from Afghanistan	2014	Ethan Kapstein	Arizona State University
Thailand's Military, the USA and China: Understanding How the Thai Military Perceives the Great Powers and Implications for the US Rebalance	2014	John Blaxland	Australian National University
Understanding American Muslims Converts in the Contexts of Security and Society	2014	John Horgan	Georgia State University

continued

TABLE C-1 Continued

Grant Title	Year of Grant	Principal Investigator	Principal Investigator's Affiliation (at the time of the National Academies study)
Taking Development (Im)balance Seriously: Using New Approaches to Measure and Model State Fragility	2014	Jonathan Moyer	University of Denver
Complex Emergencies and Political Stability in Asia	2014	Joshua Busby	University of Texas, Austin
Political Language and Crisis: A Computational Analysis of Social Disequilibrium and Security Threats	2014	Leah Windsor	University of Memphis
Preventing the Next Generation: Mapping the Pathways of Child Mobilization into VEOs	2014	Mia Bloom	Georgia State University
Tracking Critical-Mass Outbreaks in Social Contagions	2014	Michael Macy	Cornell University
Aiding Resilience? The Impact of Foreign Assistance on the Dynamics of Intrastate Armed Conflict	2014	Paul Huth	University of Maryland
Culture in Power Transitions: Sino-American Conflict in the 21st Century	2014	Robert Jervis	Columbia University
Understanding the Origin, Characteristics, and Implications of Mass Political Movements	2014	Stephen Kosack	University of Washington
Household Formation Systems, Marriage Markets, and Societal Resilience	2014	Valerie Hudson	Texas A and M University
Mobilizing Media: A Deep and Comparative Analysis of Magazines, Music, and Videos in the Context of Terrorism	2015	Anthony Lemieux	Georgia State University
Radicalization and Deradicalization of German Neo Nazis	2015	Arie Kruglanski	University of Maryland
Spheres of Influence and Regional Orders: Assessing Approaches for Responding to China's Rise	2015	Charles Glaser	George Washington University

Pilot: Security Assessment Framework for E-Residency	2015	Eric Burger	Georgetown University
New Analytics for Measuring and Countering Social Influence and Persuasion of Extremist Groups	2015	Hasan Davulcu	Arizona State University
Western Jihadism Project - Data Collection: Tracking 20 years of Al Qaeda-Inspired Terrorist Offenders and Incidents	2015	Jyette Klausen	Brandeis University
Dynamic Statistical Network Informatics	2015	Kathleen Carley	Carnegie Mellon University
Data Expansion: International Crisis Behavior Update, 2008–2013	2015	Kyle Beardsley	Duke University
Trafficking/Terrorism Nexus in Eurasia	2015	Mariya Omelicheva	University of Kansas
Global Vulnerability Markets: Using Dynamic Simulations to Change the Discovery, Supply, Demand, and Use of Vulnerabilities	2015	Michael Siegel	Massachusetts Institute of Technology
The Social Ecology of Radicalization: A Foundation for the Design of CVE Initiatives and Their Evaluation	2015	Noemie Bouhana	University College London (UK)
Ambiguous and Information Warfare in a Russian and Chinese Age[a]	2015	Patrick Porter	University of Exeter (UK)
Identity Claims: Expanding the Issue Correlates of War (ICOW) Dataset	2015	Paul Hensel	University of North Texas
The Social and Neurological Construction of Martyrdom	2015	Robert Pape	University of Chicago
Understanding China's Efforts to Become a Global Defense Science, Technology, and Innovation Leader	2015	Tai Ming Cheung	University of California, San Diego
A Computational Model of Resources and Resiliency: Deploying the Elements of National Power for Strategic Influence	2015	Tony Rivera	Duke University
Pilot: Intl University Research Ventures: Implications for US Economic Competitiveness and National Security	2015	Zachary Taylor	Georgia Institute of Technology
The Effect of Shocks on Overlapping and Functionally Interacting Social and Political Networks: A Multi-Method Approach	2015	Zeev Maoz	University of California, Davis
Refugee Flows and Instability	2016	Alex Braithwaite	University of Arizona
A Nested Mixed-Model Approach to Armed Non-State Actor Governance and Rule of Law	2016	Enrique Arias	George Mason University

continued

115

TABLE C-1 Continued

Grant Title	Year of Grant	Principal Investigator	Principal Investigator's Affiliation (at the time of the National Academies study)
Russian, Chinese, Militant, and Ideologically Extremist Messaging Effects on United States Favorability Perceptions in Central Asia	2016	Eric McGlinchey	George Mason University
The Dynamics of Common Knowledge on Social Networks: An Experimental Approach	2016	Gizem Korkmaz	Virginia Polytechnic Institute and State University
Strategic Dynamics of Cyber Conflict	2016	Jason Healey	Columbia University
Spectral Models of Security	2016	Joshua Blumenstock	University of California, Berkeley
Rising Power Alliances and the Threat of a Parallel Global Order	2016	Kelly Gallagher	Tufts University
Program on Security Institutions and Violent Instability	2016	Leonardo Arriola	University of California, Berkeley
Assessing the International Risk to National Economies Posed by a Marine Chokepoint Shutdown	2016	Lincoln Pratson	Duke University
Spatio-temporal Game Theory and Real Time Machine Learning for Adversarial Groups in the Wild	2016	Milind Tambe	University of Southern California
Africa's Youth Bulge and National Security: The Social Roots of Radicalization	2016	Parfait Eloundou-Enyegue	Cornell University
Armed Conflict Beyond Insurgency and Counterinsurgency: Comparative Evidence from Latin America and South Asia	2016	Paul Staniland	University of Chicago
Refugee Psychology and Its Potential for Refugee Radicalization	2017	Arie Kruglanski	University of Maryland
Examining Oxytocin as a Causal Mechanism for Long-Term Bonding between Humans and Autonomy	2017	Frank Krueger	George Mason University
The Warfighter's Tolerance for Autonomy and Its Importance in Strategy and Systems Development	2017	Jai Galliott	University of New South Wales

Displace, Return and Reconstruct: Population Movement and Resilience to Instability	2017	James Walsh	University of North Carolina, Charlotte
All Intervention Is Local: Understanding Government Responses to International Intervention	2017	Jessica Piombo	Naval Postgraduate School
Organizational Implications of Autonomy-Mediated Interaction	2017	Jonathan Gratch	University of Southern California
What Actions Deter? Moving from Theory to Causal Understanding of Shaping Decision Calculus	2017	Jonathan Wilkenfeld	University of Maryland
Data-Driven Learning Techniques for Cyber-Physical Situation Awareness in Defense Systems	2017	Kyriakos VamVoudakis	Virginia Polytechnic Institute and State University
Informal Economies and Societal Stability in China and Russia	2017	Marina Zaloznaya	University of Iowa
Forensic Archeology for Cyber Attribution	2017	Matthew Elder	Johns Hopkins University Applied Physics Laboratory
The Political, Economic, and Social Effects of America's Overseas Military Presence	2017	Michael Allen	Boise State University
The Disruptive Effects of Autonomy: Ethics, Trust and Organizational Decision-Making	2017	Michael Horowitz	University of Pennsylvania
Bio-Markers and Counter-Messages: Measuring Individual Differences in the Influence of Extremist Propaganda and Counter-Messages	2017	Neil Shortland	University of Massachusetts, Lowell
Integrating Structural Theories of Revolution with Evolutionary Models to Predict Societal Resilience and (In)stability	2017	Sergey Gavrilets	University of Tennessee, Knoxville
Power Projection, Deterrence Strategies and Escalation Dynamics in an Era of Challenging Near Peers, Rogue States, and Terrorist and Insurgent Organizations	2017	Steven Lobell	University of Utah

[a] The committee learned after the evaluation was completed that this grant had been cancelled due to delays associated with the Institutional Review Board process.

Appendix D

Interview Protocol for Individual Interviews with Current and Former Minerva Research Initiative Staff

DATA COLLECTION METHODS

Interviews with Department of Defense staff and former staff associated with the Minerva Research Initiative were conducted using the semistructured interview guide below. Fourteen interviews were conducted by National Academies staff between September 4 and October 8, 2018. Interviews lasted between 40 minutes and 2 hours. For further discussion of the interviews, see Chapter 2.

INTERVIEW GUIDE

1. In a few words, how would you describe your involvement with the Minerva program?

2. Minerva has been around for about 10 years and supported a lot of research. First, we want to get your quick reactions to a couple of questions. In just a few words . . .
   a. What does Minerva do especially well?
   b. What would be your highest priorities for improving the performance of Minerva? Why?

3. In which of the following areas would you describe the Minerva program as successful and which areas would benefit from improvement.
   a. contributing to the development of policy-relevant insights and tools for the national security community
   b. expanding networks of researchers interested in national security research
   c. expanding interdisciplinary and cross-disciplinary research
   d. connecting academic researchers to policymakers (for example, within the service branches, other parts of DoD, outside of DoD, as well as the executive and legislative branches)
   e. [ASK CURRENT PROGRAM DIRECTORS ONLY] creating organizational structures and processes to advance social science research around national security

4. How would you describe the quality of the research funded by the Minerva program? What are the strengths and weaknesses?

5. How has Minerva research been used by the service branches or DoD more broadly? Please provide some examples.
   - How have the service branches or DoD used the expertise of grantees (as opposed to the specific products of their research)? Examples?
   - Should and how could the service branches and DoD make better use of Minerva research products and the expertise of Minerva grantees?

6. Now let's discuss whether the right projects are being prioritized for national security needs broadly and for each service branch or whether improvements are needed.
   - How and why do priorities differ across the Office of the Secretary, other parts of DoD, and the services branches in selecting research topics and projects for funding? How are these priorities balanced?
   - When selecting projects, do you take a portfolio perspective, considering the other projects that will be awarded in the current year and the projects that were awarded in prior years? Or, is each project considered entirely on its own strengths and weaknesses?

APPENDIX D *121*

- What is the balance between scientific merit on the one hand, and on the other hand, potential for use and alignment with the research topics in selecting individual projects to fund and the full portfolio of projects?
   - What if you get a scientifically outstanding proposal that doesn't align well with any topic?
   - Should the balance between scientific merit and potential for use be changed in selecting individual projects or building the portfolio of projects?
- How could priority setting and project selection be improved?

7. Is the Minerva program facing any challenges in generating interest among social science researchers, particularly young scholars? [IF YES]
   - What is the nature of these challenges? For example, is there a need for more quantity—more research or researchers—focused on topics of national security, or a need for better quality research or researchers, or something else?
   - What has been done so far to address these challenges and what else could be done?

8. Considering the challenges and opportunities that we have been discussing, what would you say are the one, two, or three highest priorities in terms of changes that are needed to: 1) the vision of Minerva; 2) the process for setting priorities and selecting research topics; and 3) the selection of projects that are funded considering the specific purposes of more effectively meeting contemporary, changing national security challenges as well as the needs of each service branch?

9. Besides those changes in vision, priorities, and project selection, are there one or two high priorities for changes in the structure and management of the program? If so, what are they?

[PROGRAM MANAGERS ONLY]

1. Please describe the processes that [ARO/ONR/AFOSR] is involved with in the current Minerva grant cycle. For each process, please describe the activities involved, the key participants and their roles,

and the timeline. If relevant, we would also like to learn about how and why the process operates differently across service branches, how and why it operates differently from what is intended, and how and why the process has changed over time.
a. How do you choose research topics?
b. How do you solicit submissions?
c. What is the process for reviewing the submissions (of white papers and full proposals)?
d. What is the process for selecting awardees?
e. What is the process for awarding the grants?
f. How do you manage the grants and monitor grant progress and performance?
g. How do you support dissemination activities?
h. How do you support translation activities?

Appendix E

Survey of Minerva Grantees

DATA COLLECTION METHODS

The grantee survey was a census of principal investigators (PIs) for the 102 Minerva Research Initiative grants awarded between 2008 and 2017. In the case of grants with co-PIs, one PI was selected to participate in the survey per grant. The survey was conducted by the National Opinion Research Center (NORC) at the University of Chicago between August 17 and October 1, 2018. Grantees received an email invitation to complete the survey via web. Reminders were sent by email and FedEx. Of the 102 grantees, 76 answered the survey questions, and an additional 3 answered them partially, which resulted in a 77 percent completion rate. As part of the same request, grantees were also asked to submit lists of their research outputs based on the Minerva grant. Of the 79 grantees who answered survey questions, 67 (85%) provided a list of outputs. For further discussion of the grantee survey, see Chapter 2.

FREQUENCY DISTRIBUTIONS

All results reported here show percentages among all respondents, unless otherwise noted. SKP refers to items skipped by the respondent. The survey was designed to allow respondents to skip any item they did not wish to answer. In the case of questions with a series of "Yes/No" items, missing responses were recoded as "No" in cases in which the respondent selected at least one "Yes" response (see Chapter 2 for additional detail).

Q1. Prior to applying for a Minerva grant, did you learn about the Minerva grant program in any of the following ways?

	Yes	No	SKP
University research office	29	71	-
Department of Defense (DoD) website	37	63	-
National Science Foundation	22	78	-
At a conference	34	66	-
From a colleague	79	21	-
Mailing List	21	79	-
Other, please specify	11	89	-

N=76

Q2. Do you have any experience as an investigator with federal social science grant programs other than Minerva?

Yes	71
No	29
SKP	-

N=76

If Yes to Q2

Q3. Do you have experience as an investigator with any of the following federal social science grant programs?

	Yes	No	SKP
National Science Foundation grants	76	24	-
Department of Homeland Security grants	17	83	-
Grants, other than Minerva, from the DoD service branches (e.g., Air Force, Army, or Navy)	35	65	-
Other federal social science grants, please specify	46	54	-

N=54

If Yes in Q3a

Q4. How satisfied are you with the following aspects of the Minerva grant program compared to National Science Foundation grants?

[HALF SAMPLE ASKED RESPONSE OPTIONS IN REVERSE ORDER; "MUCH/SOMEWHAT" COLUMNS COMBINE RESPONSES FROM THE SEPARATE "MUCH" AND "SOMEWHAT" COLUMNS]

	Much/ Somewhat less satisfied	Much less satisfied	Somewhat less satisfied	About the same	Somewhat more satisfied	Much more satisfied	Much/ Somewhat more satisfied	Unable to compare this aspect	SKP
Selection of important topics for research	10	2	7	37	24	29	54	-	-
White paper process	12	2	10	32	17	20	37	20	-
Full Proposal submission process and requirements	12	2	10	56	15	15	29	2	-
Communication during the proposal stage	12	2	10	51	12	22	34	2	-
Post-award grant management (e.g., incremental funding, modifications, no cost extensions, compliance with terms and conditions, etc.)	15	5	10	54	12	12	24	7	-
Institutional Review Board requirements	22	10	12	56	10	2	12	10	-
Financial and narrative grant reporting requirements	15	2	12	68	10	7	17	2	-
Post-award communication	15	5	10	37	22	22	44	5	-
Assistance with dissemination or translation of research findings	7	5	2	56	7	15	22	15	-

N=41

If Yes in Q3b

Q5. How satisfied are you with the following aspects of the Minerva grant program compared to Department of Homeland Security grants?

[HALF SAMPLE ASKED RESPONSE OPTIONS IN REVERSE ORDER; "MUCH/SOMEWHAT" COLUMNS COMBINE RESPONSES FROM THE SEPARATE "MUCH" AND "SOMEWHAT" COLUMNS]

	Much/ Somewhat less satisfied	Much less satisfied	Somewhat less satisfied	About the same	Somewhat more satisfied	Much more satisfied	Much/ Somewhat more satisfied	Unable to compare this aspect	SKP
Selection of important topics for research	11	-	11	22	44	11	56	11	-
White paper process	11	-	11	11	33	22	56	22	-
Full Proposal submission process and requirements	22	-	22	22	33	11	44	11	-
Communication during the proposal stage	22	11	11	33	22	11	33	11	-
Post-award grant management (e.g., incremental funding, modifications, no cost extensions, compliance with terms and conditions, etc.)	-	-	-	33	33	11	44	22	-
Institutional Review Board requirements	33	11	22	33	11	-	11	22	-
Financial and narrative grant reporting requirements	11	-	11	44	22	-	22	22	-
Post-award communication	11	-	11	22	44	-	44	22	-
Assistance with dissemination or translation of research findings	11	-	11	33	11	-	11	44	-

N=9

If Yes in Q3c

Q6. How satisfied are you with the following aspects of the Minerva grant program compared to grants from other DoD service branches (e.g., Air Force, Army, or Navy)?

[HALF SAMPLE ASKED RESPONSE OPTIONS IN REVERSE ORDER; "MUCH/SOMEWHAT" COLUMNS COMBINE RESPONSES FROM THE SEPARATE "MUCH" AND "SOMEWHAT" COLUMNS]

	Much/ Somewhat less satisfied	Much less satisfied	Somewhat less satisfied	About the same	Somewhat more satisfied	Much more satisfied	Much/ Somewhat more satisfied	Unable to compare this aspect	SKP
Selection of important topics for research	5	-	5	58	11	26	37	-	-
White paper process	11	-	11	58	11	21	32	-	-
Full Proposal submission process and requirements	16	-	11	58	11	16	26	-	-
Communication during the proposal stage	11	-	11	74	5	11	16	-	-
Post-award grant management (e.g., incremental funding, modifications, no cost extensions, compliance with terms and conditions, etc.)	11	-	11	53	16	5	21	16	-
Institutional Review Board requirements	11	-	11	68	11	5	16	5	-
Financial and narrative grant reporting requirements	11	-	11	53	16	16	32	5	-
Post-award communication	16	5	11	68	5	5	11	5	-
Assistance with dissemination or translation of research findings	5	-	5	58	11	5	16	21	-

N=19

Q7. For each of the following activities, did the Minerva program greatly increase, somewhat increase, or not increase at all your opportunities?

[HALF SAMPLE ASKED RESPONSE OPTIONS IN REVERSE ORDER; "MUCH/SOMEWHAT" COLUMNS COMBINE RESPONSES FROM THE SEPARATE "MUCH" AND "SOMEWHAT" COLUMNS]

	Greatly increased opportunities	Somewhat increased opportunities	Did not increase at all opportunities	Not applicable	SKP
Pursuing research in new directions related to the national security topics funded by the Minerva program	76	20	1	3	-
Expanding networks with other researchers interested in national security research	49	46	4	1	-
Participating in interdisciplinary and cross-disciplinary research	46	37	16	1	-
Providing training opportunities for students and postdoctoral scholars/fellows	53	36	5	7	-
Interacting with service branch staff (e.g., Air Force, Army, or Navy) interested in integrating basic research insights into their work	26	42	28	4	-
Interacting with other DoD staff	26	38	30	5	-
Interacting with national security policy staff in other federal agencies	22	37	34	7	-
Interacting with policymakers in the legislative branch (e.g., through congressional testimony, meetings with staff or members)	13	29	50	8	-

N=76

Q8. How many students or fellows were actively involved in your Minerva grant(s) for at least one academic quarter or semester? Please enter a number.
[OPEN-ENDED RESPONSE]

	Median	SKP
Undergraduate students	3	9
Graduate students	4	4
Postdoctoral fellows/scholars	1	14

N=76

Q9a. Did your Minerva grant(s) result in any products such as publicly available software, websites, databases, patents, licenses, or training materials? Please do not include publications or presentations as we will ask about those later.
For discussion of the results, see report text.

If Yes on Q9a
Q9b. Please list any products such as publicly available software, websites, databases, patents, licenses, or training materials that resulted from your Minerva grant(s).
[OPEN-ENDED RESPONSE]
For discussion of the results, see report text.

Q10. Has your support from the Minerva program led to additional funding for research that builds on your Minerva funded work from any of the following sources?

	Yes	No	SKP
Received additional funding from the Minerva program	38	61	1
Received additional non-Minerva funding from DoD	17	82	1
Received additional funding from another source	41	58	1

N=76

If Yes on Q10c
Q11. Did you receive additional funding for research that builds on your Minerva funded work from any of the following sources?

	Yes	No	SKP
National Science Foundation	23	77	-
Department of Homeland Security	-	100	-
Other, please specify	65	35	-

N=31

Q12. Would you say the Minerva grant program has had a positive impact, no impact, or a negative impact on each of the following. . .
[HALF SAMPLE ASKED RESPONSE OPTIONS IN REVERSE ORDER]

	Positive impact	No impact	Negative impact	Unable to say	SKP
The amount of dialogue between DoD and the social science research community as a whole?	87	5	-	8	-
The number of social science researchers with interest in national security research?	82	8	-	11	-
The amount of collaboration among researchers working on different national security research topics?	76	11	-	13	-

N=76

Q13. What challenges do you face in conducting unclassified research relevant to national security that are different from the challenges you face in conducting research in other areas?
[OPEN-ENDED RESPONSE]

Coded Open-Ended Responses	
No challenges	22
Other	17
Onerous IRB/human subject review process	12
Criticism from academic colleagues due to DoD funding	12
Access to data/ability to collect data	8
Lack of interest/understanding among other scholars	7
Reluctance of research subjects to work with American researcher or DoD grantee	7
Lack of access to classified materials	5
Lack of adoption of findings by military leaders and national security stakeholders	5
Lack of interest/understanding of social science by military leaders and national security stakeholders	4
Lack of dissemination opportunities	4
Politicization of work	1
Lack of time to conduct research	1
SKP	21

N=76

Q14. Describe any changes you would like to see to the Minerva program. [OPEN-ENDED RESPONSE]

Coded Open-Ended Responses	
Other	21
Increased funding/longer grant cycles	14
Better visibility of work/dissemination opportunities	14
More cross-project collaboration	12
None	9
Opportunities for applied research	9
Better funding allocation/timing	8
Lower administrative burden	5
Feedback on initial concepts, white papers	5
More notice for call for papers	4
Funding of ongoing projects post-award	4
Less intensive human subject and IRB requirements	4
Dedicated Minerva office staff in DoD	4
Standardization of reporting requirements across program officers	1
More demographically diverse awardees	1
SKP	22

N=76

Q15. How could DoD cultivate greater interest among young scholars in working with DoD on unclassified social science research relevant to national security?
[OPEN-ENDED RESPONSE]

Coded Open-Ended Responses, Detailed Coding Scheme	
Other	21
General outreach	18
Already cultivates enough interest	14
Category specifically for junior scholars	13
Visibility at conferences	13
Increase funding for junior scholars	9
General increase of funding	9
Award more smaller grants	5
Advertise outputs/products	5
Establish grants that pair senior and junior PI's	5
Help with translating research into policy	4
Additional funding for things like websites	3
SKP	20

N=76

Coded Open-Ended Responses, Summary Coding Scheme	
Other	46
Outreach	32
Opportunities for junior scholars	21
SKP	20

N=76

OUTPUTS. Learning about the outputs that resulted from your Minerva funded research is an important aspect of this evaluation. These outputs include peer-reviewed publications, any other publications (e.g., papers, manuscripts, reports, op-ed pieces), and presentations (e.g., conference presentations, briefings, or testimony). Although you may have been asked to provide similar information to DoD, we would like to ask you to assist our evaluation by providing up-to-date information.

To make this as convenient for you as possible, this information can be provided in three different ways. In which way would you like to submit this information?

For discussion of the results, see report text.

APPENDIX E

Q16. Did you have outputs of the following type that resulted from your Minerva grant(s)?

For discussion of the results, see report text.

If Yes in Q16a

Q17. Please list your peer-reviewed publications that resulted from a Minerva grant.
[OPEN-ENDED RESPONSE]
For discussion of the results, see report text.

If Yes in Q16b

Q18. Please list any other publications (e.g., papers, manuscripts, reports, op-ed pieces) that resulted from a Minerva grant?
[OPEN-ENDED RESPONSE]
For discussion of the results, see report text.
If Yes in Q16c

Q19. Please list any presentations (e.g., conference presentations, briefings, or testimony) that resulted from a Minerva grant.
[OPEN-ENDED RESPONSE]
For discussion of the results, see report text.

UPLOAD. Please highlight peer-reviewed publications, any other publications (e.g., papers, manuscripts, reports, op-ed pieces), and any presentations (e.g., conference presentations, briefings, or testimony) that resulted from your Minerva grant(s) on your CV and upload below.
For discussion of the results, see report text.

Appendix F

Survey of Administrators of Sponsored Research

DATA COLLECTION METHODS

The survey of administrators of sponsored research was a census of 222 administrators at academic institutions with "highest research activity" and "higher research activity" based on the Carnegie Classification of Institutions of Higher Education. The person asked to complete the survey was the director of the office of sponsored programs (or equivalent) at universities where a position of this type existed. In cases where this position did not exist, the vice president for research or dean of research was contacted. The survey was conducted by the National Opinion Research Center (NORC) at the University of Chicago between August 17 and October 1, 2018. Individuals selected to participate received an email invitation to complete the survey via web. Reminders were also sent by email. Of the 222 cases, 88 completed the survey, and an additional 18 submitted partially completed surveys. The completion rate was 48 percent. For further discussion of the survey of administrators of sponsored research, see Chapter 2.

FREQUENCY DISTRIBUTIONS

All results reported here show percentages among all respondents, unless otherwise noted. SKP refers to items skipped by the respondent. The survey was designed to allow respondents to skip any item they did not wish to answer. In the case of questions with a series of "Yes/No" items, missing responses were recoded as "No" in cases in which the respondent selected at least one "Yes" response (see Chapter 2 for additional detail).

Q1. How familiar are you with the Minerva Research Initiative, the Department of Defense's (DoD's) grant program for unclassified basic social science research?

Extremely familiar	1
Very familiar	3
Moderately familiar	22
Not too familiar	34
Not familiar at all	40
SKP	-

N=88

If Q1 = Extremely, Very, Moderately, or Not too familiar
Q2. Have you or your colleagues had any experience working with Minerva grants at this institution?

Yes	21
No	79
SKP	-

N=53

Q3. Have you or your colleagues at this institution had experience working with any of the following other unclassified federal social, psychological, and economic sciences grant programs:

	Yes	No	SKP
National Science Foundation grants	99	-	1
Department of Homeland Security grants	65	34	1
Grants, other than Minerva, from the DoD service branches (e.g., Air Force, Army, or Navy)	90	9	1
Other DoD grants, please specify	56	43	1
Other federal grants, please specify	73	26	1

N=88

If Q2 = Yes AND Q3a = Yes

Q4. How do the following aspects of the Minerva grant program compare to National Science Foundation grants?
[HALF SAMPLE ASKED RESPONSE OPTIONS IN REVERSE ORDER]

	Much/ Somewhat more challenging	Much more challenging	Somewhat more challenging	About the same	Somewhat less challenging	Much less challenging	Much/ Somewhat less challenging	Unable to compare this aspect	SKP
Proposal submission process and requirements	64	18	45	18	-	-	-	9	9
Communication during the proposal stage	36	9	27	36	-	-	-	27	-
Post-award grant management (e.g., incremental funding, modifications, no cost extensions, compliance with terms and conditions, etc.)	64	18	45	27	9	-	9	-	-
Financial and narrative reporting requirements	45	-	45	36	9	9	18	-	-
Post-award communication	27	-	27	55	9	9	18	-	-
Other award characteristics (e.g., indirect costs, etc.)	27	-	27	64	-	9	9	-	-

N=11

If Q2 = Yes AND Q3b = Yes
Q5. How do the following aspects of the Minerva grant program compare to Department of Homeland Security grants? [HALF SAMPLE ASKED RESPONSE OPTIONS IN REVERSE ORDER]

	Much/ Somewhat more challenging	Much more challenging	Somewhat more challenging	About the same	Somewhat less challenging	Much less challenging	Much/ Somewhat less challenging	Unable to compare this aspect	SKP
Proposal submission process and requirements	14	-	14	43	14	14	29	14	-
Communication during the proposal stage	14	14	-	43	14	14	29	14	-
Post-award grant management (e.g., incremental funding, modifications, no cost extensions, compliance with terms and conditions, etc.)	29	14	14	29	29	14	43	-	-
Financial and narrative reporting requirements	29	14	14	29	29	14	43	-	-
Post-award communication	14	14	-	43	29	14	43	-	-
Other award characteristics (e.g., indirect costs, etc.)	29	14	14	29	29	14	43	-	-

N=7

If Q2 = Yes AND Q3c = Yes
Q6. How do the following aspects of the Minerva grant program compare to grants from other DoD service branches (e.g., Air Force, Army, or Navy)?
[HALF SAMPLE ASKED RESPONSE OPTIONS IN REVERSE ORDER]

	Much/ Somewhat more challenging	Much more challenging	Somewhat more challenging	About the same	Somewhat less challenging	Much less challenging	Much/ Somewhat less challenging	Unable to compare this aspect	SKP
Proposal submission process and requirements	18	9	9	64	9	-	9	9	-
Communication during the proposal stage	9	9	-	64	9	-	9	9	9
Post-award grant management (e.g., incremental funding, modifications, no cost extensions, compliance with terms and conditions, etc.)	9	9	-	64	27	-	27	-	-
Financial and narrative reporting requirements	9	9	0	73	18	-	18	-	-
Post-award communication	18	9	9	64	18	-	18	-	-
Other award characteristics (e.g., indirect costs, etc.)	18	9	9	64	18	-	18	-	-

N=11

Q7. Describe any changes you would like to see to the Minerva grant program.
[OPEN-ENDED RESPONSE]
For discussion of the results, see report text.

If Q3a = Yes AND (Q3c = Yes or Q3d = Yes)
Q8. How do the following aspects of DoD grant programs in general compare to <u>NSF</u> grants?
[HALF SAMPLE ASKED RESPONSE OPTIONS IN REVERSE ORDER]

	Much/ Somewhat more challenging	Much more challenging	Somewhat more challenging	About the same	Somewhat less challenging	Much less challenging	Much/ Somewhat less challenging	Unable to compare this aspect	SKP
Proposal submission process and requirements	75	29	46	14	3	3	5	6	-
Communication during the proposal stage	51	14	37	32	6	1	8	10	-
Post-award grant management (e.g., incremental funding, modifications, no cost extensions, compliance with terms and conditions, etc.)	72	32	41	16	3	3	5	6	-
Financial and narrative reporting requirements	58	23	35	28	3	3	5	9	-
Post-award communication	56	16	39	30	3	1	4	9	1
Other award characteristics (e.g., indirect costs, etc.)	47	14	33	46	1	-	1	5	1

N=79

If Q3b = Yes AND (Q3c = Yes or Q3d = Yes)
Q9. How do the following aspects of DoD grant programs in general compare to Department of Homeland Security grants?
[HALF SAMPLE ASKED RESPONSE OPTIONS IN REVERSE ORDER]

	Much/ Somewhat more challenging	Much more challenging	Somewhat more challenging	About the same	Somewhat less challenging	Much less challenging	Much/ Somewhat less challenging	Unable to compare this aspect	SKP
Proposal submission process and requirements	15	7	7	48	17	2	19	17	2
Communication during the proposal stage	11	6	6	56	7	4	11	20	2
Post-award grant management (e.g., incremental funding, modifications, no cost extensions, compliance with terms and conditions, etc.)	15	6	9	54	13	-	13	17	2
Financial and narrative reporting requirements	13	6	7	52	9	4	13	20	2
Post-award communication	11	2	9	56	7	4	11	20	2
Other award characteristics (e.g., indirect costs, etc.)	9	2	7	59	7	4	11	19	2

N=54

Q10. Describe any changes you would like to see to DoD grant programs in general.
[OPEN-ENDED RESPONSE]

Coded Open-Ended Responses, Summary Coding Scheme	
Standardization of reporting/administrative requirements across DoD grant programs	14
Better IT systems for grant management	14
Other	13
Simpler/better guidance for application, invoicing, and reporting	10
More transparency around expectations	8
Less burdensome post-award management	4
Fewer restrictions on the use of funding	3
Better publication of funding opportunities	1
SKP	59

N=79

Q11. Aside from DoD, are you aware of agencies or organizations that provide grants for unclassified research in the social, psychological and economic sciences on topics relevant to national security (regardless of whether your institution has received such grants)?

Yes	35
No	63
SKP	2

N=88

If Q11 = Yes

Q12. What other agencies or organizations are you aware of that provide grants for unclassified research in the social, psychological and economic sciences on topics relevant to national security?
[OPEN-ENDED RESPONSE]

Coded Open-Ended Responses, Summary Coding Scheme	
Department of Homeland Security	26
Other	26
National Science Foundation	19
Department of Justice	16
National Institute of Health	10
Intelligence Advanced Research Projects Activity	6
National Security Agency	6
SKP	35

N=31

Q13. Which statement best describes your opinion, even if neither is exactly right.

Most people at my institution have favorable views of conducting unclassified national security research in general.	66
Most people at my institution have unfavorable views of conducting unclassified national security research in general.	11
Don't know.	23
SKP	-

N=88

Q14. Which statement best describes your opinion, even if neither is exactly right.

Most *social, psychological, and economic sciences faculty members* at my institution have favorable views of conducting unclassified national security research in general.	49
Most *social, psychological, and economic sciences faculty members* at my institution have unfavorable views of conducting unclassified national security research in general.	11
Don't know.	40
SKP	-

N=88

Q14a. Please provide any additional details about the views of social, psychological, and economic sciences faculty on conducting unclassified national security research.
For discussion of the results, see report text.

Q15. How could DoD cultivate greater interest among young scholars in working with DoD on unclassified social, psychological, and economic sciences research relevant to national security?
[OPEN-ENDED RESPONSE]

Coded Open-Ended Responses, Detailed Coding Scheme	
Greater visibility/awareness	15
Other	14
Opportunities for junior faculty and doctoral awards	10
Campus visits	9
More support for proposals/simpler proposal process	7
More resources to promote DoD opportunities	6
More webinars	5
Increase presence at conferences	3
Broaden type of research accepted	2
SKP	53

N=88

Coded Open-Ended Responses, Summary Coding Scheme	
Outreach	20
Other	20
Opportunities for junior scholars	10
SKP	53

N=88

If Q1 = Extremely, Very, Moderately, or Not too familiar
Q16. Do you have any other comments for consideration by the National Academies of Sciences, Engineering, and Medicine committee tasked with evaluating the Minerva Research Initiative?
For discussion of the results, see report text.

Appendix G

Individuals Who Provided Input during the Committee's Public Meetings[1]

Eli Berman, University of California, San Diego
Kathleen Carley, Carnegie Mellon University
David Chu, Institute for Defense Analyses
Matthew Clark, Science and Technology Directorate, Department of Homeland Security
Hasan Davulcu, Arizona State University
Michael Desch, University of Notre Dame
Thomas Fingar, Stanford University
Erin Fitzgerald, University of Maryland
James Goldgeier, Council on Foreign Relations
Gerald (Jay) Goodwin, Foundational Science Research Unit, U.S. Army Research Institute
Christina Hegadorn, United States Institute of Peace
David Honey, Office of the Director of National Intelligence
Benjamin Knott, Air Force Office of Scientific Research, Department of Defense
Gary Kollmorgen, GSK Inc.
Natalie Konopinski, American Anthropological Association
Martin Kruger, Office of Naval Research, Department of Defense
Thomas Mahnken, Center of Strategic and Budgetary Assessments
Laura McNamara, Sandia National Laboratories (via webconferencing)
Thomas McNaugher, Georgetown University

---

[1] Public meetings were held on January 16, April 12, July 19, and October 2, 2018.

David Montgomery, Department of Defense
Bindu Nair, Department of Defense
Steve Newell, American Psychological Association
Kaleb Redden, Office of the Under Secretary of Defense for Policy, Department of Defense
Steven Riskin, United States Institute of Peace
Adam Russell, Defense Sciences Office, Defense Advanced Research Projects Agency
Betsy Super, American Political Science Association
Alan Tomkins, Division of Behavioral and Cognitive Sciences, National Science Foundation
Lisa Troyer, Army Research Office, Department of Defense
James Walsh, University of North Carolina, Charlotte

Appendix H

Output Categories and Coding Notes

Output Type	Notes on Coding
1. Peer-reviewed publications	Journals in which the articles appeared were designated as peer-reviewed if they were considered to be peer-reviewed in any of three library databases that contain peer-reviewed journals: Scopus, Proquest, and Ulrich's. Publications were included in this category if they were published, or were described by principal investigators (PIs) as "in press," "forthcoming," "to appear in," "being copyedited," "conditionally accepted," or "under contract." (If publications were described as in progress in various alternative ways, they were coded as such.)
2. Other publications	Included non-peer-reviewed journal articles, papers, paper series, working papers, reports, op-ed pieces, blogs, and newsletters. Also see above note on publication status.
3. Books and book chapters	All books and book chapters, regardless of peer-review status. Also see above note on publication status.
4. Conference proceedings	All conference proceedings, regardless of peer-review status.
5. "In-progress" publications	Included articles written for peer-reviewed or non-peer-reviewed journals, or books and book chapters that were described by the PIs as "revise and resubmit," "under review or submitted to," "typescript," "manuscript," "draft available," "draft in progress," or "being reviewed by PI."
6. Presentations	Included conference presentations, briefings, or testimony.
7. Products	Included sharable resources, such as publicly available software, websites, databases, patents, licenses, or training materials.

Appendix I

Publications and Presentations by Year

TABLE I-1 Publications and Presentations by Year (rounded to nearest whole number)

Numbers Across All Years	Total (n = 1,204) Range	Total Median	Peer-reviewed Publications (n = 152) Range	Peer-reviewed Median	Other Publications (n = 333) Range	Other Median	Books/Chapters (n = 62) Range	Books/Chapters Median	Conference Proceedings (n = 28) Range	Conference Median	In-Progress Publications (n = 47) Range	In-Progress Median	Presentations (n = 582) Range	Presentations Median
All Years: 57 PIs reported 1204 outputs	1–133	10	0–18	2	0–124	1	0–12	0	0–18	0	0–7	0	0–80	5
2009 3 PIs reported 236 outputs	1–124	111	0–18	0	0–124	30	0–12	0	0–3	0	0–1	0	0–46	0
2010 12 PIs reported 129 outputs	1–30	8	0–5	2.5	0–3	0	0–2	0	0	0	0–1	0	0–23	5.5
2012 5 PIs reported 237 outputs	9–133	24	0–5	4	0–38	1	0–9	1	0	0	0–2	1	1–80	17
2013 7 PIs reported 187 outputs	16–37	26	0–15	5	0–8	2	0–11	1	0–1	0	0–7	0	0–27	14
2014 8 PIs reported 189 outputs	3–45	20.5	0–7	2.0	1–22	3	0–6	0	0	0	0–4	0	0–29	9
2015 10 PIs reported 113 outputs	2–32	7.5	0–6	2.0	0–4	1	0–3	.5	0–18	0	0–4	0	0–17	3
2016 7 PIs reported 87 outputs	2–52	6	0–2	0	0–16	0	0	0	0–2	0	0–6	0	0–29	4
2017 5 PIs reported 26 outputs	1–9	6	0–4	0	0–3	0	0–1	0	0–4	0	0–2	0	0–7	1

NOTE: PI = principal investigator.

Appendix J

Impact Metrics of Journals in Which Minerva Principal Investigators Reported Publishing (Table J-1) and Journals without Journal-Level Impact Factor Scores in Which Minerva Principal Investigators Published (Table J-2)

TABLE J-1 Impact Metrics of Journals in Which Minerva Principal Investigators Reported Publishing

Journal	Number of Minerva Papers	Subject Fields[a]	2017 CiteScore	CiteScore Rank	CiteScore Percentile	2017 SJR Score	SJR Rank	SJR Quartile
1. *American Political Science Review*	1	A. Political Science and International Relations	3.77	4/436	99th	5.587	7/466	Q1
2. *International Organization*	2	B. Sociology and Political Science	4.93	10/1029	99th	8.527	3/1104	Q1
3. *Journal of Personality and Social Psychology*	1	B. Sociology and Political Science	6.40	4/1029	99th	4.302	15/1104	Q1
4. *Pediatrics*	1	G. Pediatrics, Perinatology and Child Health	5.15	3/271	99th	3.337	2/301	Q1
5. *World Politics*	1	A. Political Science and International Relations	4.21	3/436	99th	6.544	5/466	Q1
6. *Annual Review of Political Science*	3	B. Sociology and Political Science	4.81	11/1029	98th	5.109	11/1104	Q1
7. *British Journal of Political Science*	1	B. Sociology and Political Science	3.96	18/1029	98th	4.661	12/1104	Q1
8. *IEEE Transactions on Neural Networks and Learning Systems*	1	C. Computer Science Applications	8.96	7/535	98th	3.406	10/2290	Q1
9. *Journal of Peace Research*	10	A. Political Science and International Relations	3.40	8/436	98th	3.888	11/466	Q1
10. *Political Psychology*	1	A. Political Science and International Relations	3.45	7/436	98th	2.260	22/466	Q1

11.	Population and Development Review	1	E. Demography	3.13	2/87	98th	2.324	2/94	Q1
12.	Security Dialogue	1	A. Political Science and International Relations	3.48	6/436	98th	2.389	18/466	Q1
13.	World Development	1	B. Sociology and Political Science	3.92	19/1029	98th	2.122	54/1104	Q1
14.	Journal of Political Economy	1	K. Economics and Econometrics	4.93	17/565	97th	16.309	5/613	Q1
15.	Post-Soviet Affairs	1	A. Political Science and International Relations	3.11	10/436	97th	2.411	17/466	Q1
16.	IEEE Transactions on Automatic Control	1	C. Control and Systems Engineering	5.90	9/224	96th	3.433	3/948	Q1
17.	International Security	6	F. Law	2.53	18/529	96th	4.005	3/602	Q1
18.	Journal of Conflict Resolution	10	A. Political Science and International Relations	2.84	15/436	96th	4.037	9/466	Q1
19.	Psychological Science	1	G. General Psychology	6.17	7/189	96th	4.128	7/241	Q1
20.	IEEE Transactions on Knowledge and Data Engineering	1	C. Computer Science Applications	5.45	26/535	95th	1.133	84/2290	Q1
21.	Proceedings of the National Academy of Sciences of the United States of America	1	D. Multidisciplinary	8.59	4/87	95th	6.092	3/116	Q1
22.	Social Cognitive and Affective Neuroscience	1	G. Experimental and Cognitive Psychology	3.90	6/125	95th	2.078	12/137	Q1

continued

153

TABLE J-1 Continued

Journal	Number of Minerva Papers	Subject Fields[a]	2017 CiteScore	CiteScore Rank	CiteScore Percentile	2017 SJR Score	SJR Rank	SJR Quartile
23. *Politics and Religion*	1	M. Religious Studies	0.59	22/389	94th	0.541	9/432	Q1
24. *Scientific Reports*	3	D. Multidisciplinary	4.36	5/87	94th	1.533	5/116	Q1
25. *American Psychologist*	1	G. General Psychology	3.83	12/189	93rd	1.594	23/241	Q1
26. *Terrorism and Political Violence*	2	A. Political Science and International Relations	2.12	30/436	93rd	1.163	51/466	Q1
27. *International Migration Review*	1	E. Demography	2.54	7/87	92nd	1.641	7/94	Q1
28. *Journal of Politics*	1	B. Sociology and Political Science	2.53	81/1029	92nd	4.220	16/1104	Q1
29. *Perspectives on Politics*	2	A. Political Science and International Relations	2.08	31/436	92nd	2.075	25/466	Q1
30. *IEEE Transactions on Visualization and Computer Graphics*	1	C. Computer Graphics and Computer-Aided Design	4.10	6/65	91st	0.869	15/449	Q1
31. *PLoS ONE*	1	L. General Agricultural and Biological Sciences	3.01	16/177	91st	1.164	31/268	Q1
32. *SIAM Journal of Scientific Computing*	1	C. Applied Mathematics	2.61	37/423	91st	1.973	33/514	Q1
33. *African Affairs*	1	B. Sociology and Political Science	2.27	102/1029	90th	1.869	64/1104	Q1
34. *Contemporary Islam*	8	M. Religious Studies	0.42	41/389	89th	0.130	162/432	Q2

35.	*Daedalus*	1	J. History and Philosophy of Science	1.19	14/126	89th	0.421	34/145	Q1
36.	*Organizational Behavior and Human Decision Processes*	1	I. Organizational Behavior and Human Resource Management	3.09	18/173	89th	1.989	13/194	Q1
37.	*Psychology of Violence*	1	G. Health (social violence)	2.40	25/241	89th	1.427	14/281	Q1
38.	*Journal of Human Rights*	1	F. Law	1.41	59/529	88th	0.451	158/602	Q2
39.	*Security Studies*	2	A. Political Science and International Relations	1.77	48/436	88th	1.801	28/466	Q1
40.	*Studies in Conflict and Terrorism*	4	A. Political Science and International Relations	1.77	48/436	88th	0.913	65/466	Q1
41.	*Journal of Ethnic and Migration Studies*	2	E. Demography	2.11	11/87	87th	1.486	10/94	Q1
42.	*Conflict Management and Peace Science*	2	A. Political Science and International Relations	1.39	65/436	85th	2.441	16/466	Q1
43.	*International Journal of Intercultural Relations*	2	B. Sociology and Political Science	1.86	149/1029	85th	0.732	226/1104	Q1
44.	*Transactions in GIS*	1	L. General Earth and Planetary Sciences	2.33	27/182	85th	0.723	68/323	Q1
45.	*Washington Quarterly*	3	F. Law	1.28	79/529	85th	1.102	55/602	Q1
46.	*Foreign Policy Analysis*	2	A. Political Science and International Relations	1.32	70/436	83rd	1.425	36/466	Q1
47.	*Demographic Research*	1	E. Demography	1.75	16/87	82nd	1.235	14/94	Q1
48.	*International Peacekeeping*	1	A. Political Science and International Relations	1.26	76/436	82nd	0.768	79/466	Q1

continued

155

TABLE J-1 Continued

Journal	Number of Minerva Papers	Subject Fields[a]	2017 CiteScore	CiteScore Rank	CiteScore Percentile	2017 SJR Score	SJR Rank	SJR Quartile
49. *Journal of Strategic Studies*	2	A. Political Science and International Relations	1.26	76/436	82nd	0.909	67/466	Q1
50. *Political Research Quarterly*	1	B. Sociology and Political Science	1.67	179/1029	82nd	1.595	81/1104	Q1
51. *Operations Research*	1	I. Management Science and Operations Research	2.67	26/137	81st	2.951	8/195	Q1
52. *American Journal of Orthopsychiatry*	1	D. Arts and Humanities (miscellaneous)	2.00	49/249	80th	0.909	70/400	Q1
53. *Foreign Affairs*	2	A. Political Science and International Relations	1.14	89/436	79th	0.721	83/466	Q1
54. *International Journal of Adaptive Control and Signal Processing*	1	C. Electrical and Electronic Engineering	2.48	135/644	79th	0.915	93/2352	Q1
55. *Journal of Development Studies*	1	D. Development	1.66	40/204	79th	0.926	35/227	Q1
56. *Dynamics of Asymmetric Conflict: Pathways toward Terrorism and Genocide*	1	H. Cultural Studies	0.52	166/771	78th	0.121	480/876	Q3
57. *Social Science Quarterly*	1	D. General Social Sciences	1.15	45/213	78th	0.763	87/497	Q1
58. *Al-Jami'ah*	2	D. General Arts and Humanities	0.23	28/122	77th	0.124	287/400	Q3

59.	Network Science	1	B. Sociology and Political Science	1.36	229/1029	77th	0.461	343/1104	Q2
60.	Social Network Analysis and Mining	1	C. Media Technology	1.24	15/65	77th	0.306	23/216	Q1
61.	International Interactions: Empirical and Theoretical Research in International Relations	3	A. Political Science and International Relations	1.01	102/436	76th	1.382	39/466	Q1
62.	International Migration	1	E. Demography	1.28	22/87	75th	0.887	22/94	Q1
63.	Asian Journal of Social Psychology	2	D. General Social Sciences	0.94	58/213	73rd	0.465	143/497	Q2
64.	Criminology & Public Policy	2	I. Public Administration	1.76	32/117	73rd	1.473	15/130	Q1
65.	Computer Law and Security Review	1	F. Law	0.78	156/529	70th	0.334	214/602	Q2
66.	Journal of East Asian Studies	1	A. Political Science and International Relations	0.79	143/436	66th	0.590	97/466	Q1
67.	Journal of Optimization Theory and Applications	1	C. Control and Optimization	1.30	25/73	66th	0.813	19/291	Q1
68.	Computer Journal	1	C. General Computer Science	1.10	72/195	63rd	0.319	101/548	Q2
69.	Race and Justice	1	H. Anthropology	0.58	116/313	62nd	0.417	87/349	Q2
70.	Public Choice	3	K. Economics and Econometrics	1.07	243/565	57th	0.991	163/613	Q2

continued

157

TABLE J-1 Continued

Journal	Number of Minerva Papers	Subject Fields[a]	2017 CiteScore	CiteScore Rank	CiteScore Percentile	2017 SJR Score	SJR Rank	SJR Quartile
71. The Australian Journal of Anthropology	1	H. Anthropology	0.51	133/313	57th	0.291	128/349	Q2
72. Journal of Politics in Latin America	1	A. Political Science and International Relations	0.57	191/436	56th	0.209	264/466	Q3
73. International Area Studies Review	1	A. Political Science and International Relations	0.54	194/436	55th	0.345	176/466	Q2
74. East West Center Asia Pacific Issues	1	A. Political Science and International Relations	0.53	197/436	54th	0.200	277/466	Q3
75. International Negotiation	1	A. Political Science and International Relations	0.52	204/436	53rd	0.431	141/466	Q2
76. Sojourn: Journal of Social Issues in Southeast Asia	1	H. Anthropology	0.41	155/313	50th	0.294	125/349	Q2
77. Journal of North African Studies	1	A. Political Science and International Relations	0.47	217/436	49th	0.363	169/466	Q2
78. Social Choice and Welfare	1	D. Social Sciences (misc.)	0.65	124/226	45th	0.644	104/497	Q1
79. Orbis	1	B. Sociology and Political Science	0.42	569/1029	44th	0.215	622/1104	Q3
80. Risk, Hazards and Crisis in Public Policy	1	I. Public Administration	0.50	87/117	26th	0.153	107/130	Q4

81. *Review of Middle East Studies*	1	J. History	0.04	799/983	16th	0.101	837/1120	Q4
82. *Commonwealth Law Bulletin*	1	F. Law	0.07	473/529	10th	0.102	538/602	Q4
Total	138						

NOTE: SJR = Scimago Journal Ranking.

^aColumn 3 of this table contains for each journal a subject field to which it is assigned by Scopus (2019g). These subject fields are important for classifying content and making comparisons. (The letters in front of the subject field were used to collapse fields for Table 4-3 in the main text.)

159

TABLE J-2 Journals without Journal-Level Impact Factor Scores in Which Minerva Principal Investigators Published

Journal	Number of Articles	Peer-Reviewed
1. Behavioral Science & Policy	1	Yes
2. East Asia Forum Quarterly	1	Yes
3. Georgetown Journal of International Affairs	1	Yes
4. Heritage of Islam Nusantara: International Journal of Religious Literature and Heritage	1	Yes
5. International Journal of Semantic Computing	1	Yes
6. Journal of Cybersecurity	2	Yes
7. Laws	1	Yes
8. Research and Politics	2	Yes
9. RIMA: Review of Indonesian and Malaysian Affairs	1	Yes
10. Scientia Militaria - South African Journal of Military Studies	1	Yes
11. Strategic Studies Quarterly	1	Yes
12. The Economics of Peace and Security Journal	1	Yes
13. The Georgetown Security Studies Review	1	No
14. Academy of Science and Engineering (ASE) Human Journal	2	No
15. AEA Paper and Proceedings	1	No
16. Africa Yearbook	2	No
17. Armed Conflict Survey	1	No
18. COMOPS Journal	19	No
19. En Arche: Indonesian Journal of Inter-Religious Studies	1	No
20. International Journal of Interreligious and Intercultural Relations	1	No
21. Journal of Baltic Security Studies	1	No
22. Journal of Financial Transformation	1	No
23. Journal of Information Warfare	1	No
24. Oxford Monitor of Forced Migration: Field Monitor	1	No
25. Perspectives on Terrorism	1	No
26. Political Science Research and Methods	1	No
27. Prism Journal	3	No
28. SAIS Review	1	No
29. The Citizen	1	No
30. West African Papers OECD special series	2	No
Total	55	30
Total Peer Reviewed	14	12
Total Not Peer-Reviewed	41	18

Appendix K

Field-Weighted Citation Impact of Publications Reported by Principal Investigators

TABLE K-1 Field-Weighted Citation Impact of Publications Reported by Principal Investigators

Article Number	Year Article Published	Number of Citations Received	Benchmarking Percentile	Subject Field Relative to Percentile	Field-Weighted Citation Impact
1	2014	247	99	Political Science and International Relations	40.93
2	2017	28	99	Public Administration	11.19
3	2014	102	99	Political Science and International Relations	10.80
4	2011	148	99	Economics, Econometrics, and Finance	10.34
5	2013	81	99	Political Science and International Relations	9.85
6	2013	72	99	Law	8.80
7	2011	72	99	Political Science and International Relations	7.38
8	2016	18	99	Political Science and International Relations	6.93
9	2015	23	99	Political Science and International Relations	4.50
10	2012	70	98	Political Science and International Relations	10.16
11	2014	35	98	Political Science and International Relations	8.06
12	2014	30	97	Political Science and International Relations	4.59
13	2015	19	96	Sociology and Political Science	7.26
14	2014	29	96	Sociology and Political Science	5.09
15	2016	24	96	Psychology	4.52
16	2015	6	96	Religious Studies	3.71
17	2015	25	95	Political Science and International Relations	5.72
18	2014	31	95	Social Sciences	4.00
19	2015	47	95	Social Sciences	3.53
20	2015	31	94	Medicine	4.29

21	2014	5	Social Sciences	12.98
22	2017	15	Social Sciences	8.19
23	2016	7	Political Science and International Relations	2.27
24	2015	10	Political Science and International Relations	2.38
25	2018	12	Medicine	14.16
26	2015	22	Mathematics	3.48
27	2014	12	Political Science and International Relations	3.16
28	2016	17	Computer Science	2.60
29	2017	4	Political Science and International Relations	2.22
30	2015	8	Political Science and International Relations	2.17
31	2015	11	Economics, Econometrics, and Finance	2.09
32	2009	29	Political Science and International Relations	2.05
33	2012	18	Political Science and International Relations	1.90
34	2017	10	Arts and Humanities	2.98
35	2017	4	Political Science and International Relations	2.78
36	2013	5	Religious Studies	2.49
37	2011	20	Political Science and International Relations	2.15
38	2013	16	Arts and Humanities	1.64
39	2016	9	Political Science and International Relations	2.27
40	2017	4	Political Science and International Relations	2.03
41	2016	7	Political Science and International Relations	2.63
42	2011	14	Political Science and International Relations	2.61

continued

TABLE K-1 Continued

Article Number	Year Article Published	Number of Citations Received	Benchmarking Percentile	Subject Field Relative to Percentile	Field-Weighted Citation Impact
43	2014	9	82	Political Science and International Relations	2.58
44	2013	20	80	Medicine	2.40
45	2017	1	80	Social Sciences	1.96
46	2016	9	80	Arts and Humanities	1.55
47	2017	2	75	Sociology and Political Science	2.61
48	2016	4	75	Sociology and Political Science	1.90
49	2014	3	75	Religious Studies	1.66
50	2016	5	75	Political Science and International Relations	1.62
51	2011	14	75	Social Sciences	1.22
52	2015	29	75	Multidisciplinary	1.19
53	2014	7	75	Sociology and Political Science	1.18
54	2017	3	75	Political Science and International Relations	1.02
55	2015	2	75	Cultural Studies	0.84
56	2016	8	70	Computer Science	2.51
57	2013	7	70	Political Science and International Relations	1.01
58	2015	5	70	Social Sciences	0.73
59	2012	12	70	Social Sciences	0.65
60	2017	4	65	Law	2.78
61	2013	1	65	Psychology	1.91
62	2014	5	65	Political Science and International Relations	1.14

63	2015	4	65	Political Science and International Relations	1.09
64	2017	1	65	Political Science and International Relations	0.62
65	2017	3	60	Social Sciences	3.98
66	2015	4	60	Political Science and International Relations	1.50
67	2010	2	60	Religious Studies	0.82
68	2016	2	50	Social Sciences	1.03
69	2011	2	50	Social Sciences	0.59
70	2013	7	50	Medicine	0.58
71	2015	9	50	Multidisciplinary	0.47
72	2015	8	45	Medicine	1.67
73	2015	4	45	Political Science and International Relations	0.89
74	2015	2	45	Social Sciences	0.50
75	2011	7	45	Economics, Econometrics, and Finance	0.46
76	2015	1	45	Social Sciences	0.41
77	2015	2	45	Social Sciences	0.38
78	2016	3	45	Political Science and International Relations	0.29
79	2013	2	35	Communication	0.37
80	2015	8	35	Multidisciplinary	0.36
81	2016	2	35	Information Systems	0.33
82	2011	3	35	Anthropology	0.27
83	2014	1	30	Social Sciences	0.24
84	2012	133	not provided	not provided	16.86

continued

TABLE K-1 Continued

Article Number	Year Article Published	Number of Citations Received	Benchmarking Percentile	Subject Field Relative to Percentile	Field-Weighted Citation Impact
85	2017	6	not provided	not provided	15.31
86	2018	3	not provided	not provided	11.12
87	2019	2	not provided	not provided	9.65
88	2018	14	not provided	not provided	8.88
89	2017	11	not provided	not provided	8.29
90	2015	3	not provided	not provided	6.46
91	2018	1	not provided	not provided	5.32
92	2018	3	not provided	not provided	5.31
93	2017	1	not provided	not provided	4.85
94	2017	10	not provided	not provided	4.68
95	2015	22	not provided	not provided	4.38
96	2018	1	not provided	not provided	3.80
97	2016	11	not provided	not provided	3.59
98	2017	2	not provided	not provided	2.89
99	2017	3	not provided	not provided	1.64
100	2018	1	not provided	not provided	1.60
101	2018	2	not provided	not provided	1.60
102	2016	4	not provided	not provided	1.38
103	2018	2	not provided	not provided	1.31
104	2017	5	not provided	not provided	1.27

105	2017	1	not provided	not provided	0.68
106	2015	1	not provided	not provided	0.00
107	2016	0	not provided	not provided	0.00
108	2016	0	not provided	not provided	0.00
109	2016	0	not provided	not provided	0.00
110	2017	0	not provided	not provided	0.00
111	2017	0	not provided	not provided	0.00
112	2017	0	not provided	not provided	0.00
113	2017	0	not provided	not provided	0.00
114	2017	0	not provided	not provided	0.00
115	2017	0	not provided	not provided	0.00
116	2017	0	not provided	not provided	0.00
117	2018	0	not provided	not provided	0.00
118	2018	0	not provided	not provided	0.00
119	2018	0	not provided	not provided	0.00
120	2018	0	not provided	not provided	0.00
121	2018	0	not provided	not provided	0.00
122	2018	0	not provided	not provided	0.00
123	2018	1	not provided	not provided	0.00
124	2019	0	not provided	not provided	0.00
125	2019	0	not provided	not provided	0.00

Appendix L

Universities with Minerva Grants

TABLE L-1 Universities with Minerva Grants: Classification of Research Institution Type Based on Carnegie Classification of Institutions of Higher Education

University	Number of Minerva Grants	Institution with Highest Research Activity	Institution with Higher Research Activity	Institution with Moderate Research Activity	Minority-Serving Institution
1. Arizona State University-Tempe	2	x			
2. Brandeis University	1	x			
3. Brown University	1	x			
4. Carnegie Mellon University	2	x			
5. Columbia University in the City of New York	3	x			
6. Cornell University	2	x			
7. Duke University	4	x			
8. George Mason University	3	x			
9. George Washington University	1	x			
10. Georgetown University	1	x			
11. Georgia Institute of Technology–Main Campus	1	x			
12. Georgia State University	3	x			
13. Harvard University–Boston Children's Hospital	1	x			
14. Johns Hopkins University	1	x			
15. Massachusetts Institute of Technology	3	x			
16. Ohio State University–Main Campus	1	x			
17. Pennsylvania State University–Main Campus	1	x			
18. Princeton University	1	x			

19. Rutgers University–New Brunswick	1	x	
20. Stanford University	2	x	
21. Texas A & M University–College Station	2	x	
22. The University of Tennessee-Knoxville	2	x	
23. The University of Texas at Arlington	1	x	x
24. The University of Texas at Austin	2	x	
25. Tufts University	2	x	
26. University of Arizona	1	x	
27. University of California–Berkeley	3	x	
28. University of California–Davis	1	x	
29. University of California–Los Angeles	2	x	
30. University of California–San Diego	7	x	
31. University of Chicago	3	x	
32. University of Colorado Boulder	1	x	
33. University of Florida	1	x	
34. University of Illinois at Urbana-Champaign	1	x	
35. University of Iowa	2	x	
36. University of Kansas	2	x	
37. University of Maryland–College Park	7	x	x
38. University of North Texas	1	x	
39. University of Pennsylvania	1	x	
40. University of Southern California	2	x	x

continued

TABLE L-1 Continued

University	Number of Minerva Grants	Institution with Highest Research Activity	Institution with Higher Research Activity	Institution with Moderate Research Activity	Minority-Serving Institution
41. University of Utah	1	x			
42. University of Virginia–Main Campus	2	x			
43. University of Washington–Seattle Campus	1	x			
44. University of Wisconsin–Madison	1	x			
45. Virginia Commonwealth University	1	x			
46. Virginia Polytechnic Institute and State University	2	x			
47. College of William and Mary	1		x		
48. Naval Postgraduate School	3		x		
49. The New School	1		x		
50. University of Denver	1		x		
51. University of Massachusetts–Lowell	1		x		
52. University of Memphis	1		x		x
53. University of North Carolina at Charlotte	2		x		
54. Arizona State University–Downtown Phoenix	1			x	x
55. Boise State University	1			x	
56. San Francisco State University	1			x	
Total Number of Institutions	56	46	10	3	5

Universities without Carnegie Research Classification	
57. Middlebury Institute of International Studies	1
58. Australian National University (AU)	2
59. King's College, London (UK)	1
60. University College, London (UK)	1
61. University of Exeter (UK)	1
62. University of Guelph (CA)	1
63. University of New South Wales (AU)	1
64. University of Queensland (AU)	1
Total Number of Institutions	9

Appendix M

Biographical Sketches of Committee Members and Staff

Allen L. Schirm (*Chair*) retired from Mathematica Policy Research after holding several positions, including vice president, director of human services research, director of methods, and senior fellow. He has extensive experience conducting evaluations and deriving statistical estimates pertaining to federal and state programs for food and nutrition assistance, as well as education and other support programs for at-risk youth. He is a National Associate of the National Academies of Sciences, Engineering, and Medicine and has contributed to 16 National Academies reports as a chair and committee member, including as chair of the Panel on Estimating Children Eligible for School Nutrition Programs Using the American Community Survey and as a member of the Committee on Affordability of National Flood Insurance Program Premiums. He is a fellow of the American Statistical Association (ASA) and former chair of the ASA Social Statistics Section. He has a Ph.D. in economics from the University of Pennsylvania.

Burt S. Barnow is Amsterdam professor of public service and of economics at George Washington University. Previously, he was associate director for research at Johns Hopkins University's Institute for Policy Studies; on the staff of the Lewin Group; and at the U.S. Department of Labor, including 4 years as director of the Office of Research and Evaluation in the Employment and Training Administration. He has extensive experience conducting research on implementation of large government programs and has published widely in the fields of labor economics and evaluation. He has served on many committees of the National Academies of Sciences, Engineering, and Medicine, including the Committee for the Context of

Military Environments: Social and Organizational Factors; the Committee on Science, Technology, Engineering and Mathematics Workforce Needs for the U.S. Department of Defense and the U.S. Defense Industrial Base. He has a Ph.D. in economics from the University of Wisconsin–Madison.

Karen S. Cook is the Ray Lyman Wilbur professor of sociology, director of the Institute for Research in the Social Sciences, and vice provost for faculty development and diversity at Stanford University. She conducts research on social exchange networks, power and influence dynamics, intergroup relations, negotiation strategies, social justice, and trust in social relations. Her research underscores the importance of trust in facilitating exchange relationships and of networks in creating social capital. She is a recipient of the Social Psychology Section Cooley Mead Award for Career Contributions to Social Psychology of the American Sociological Association. She is a member of the National Academy of Sciences, the American Academy of Arts and Sciences, the Board of Trustees of the Russell Sage Foundation, and the Advisory Committee for the Directorate for Social, Behavioral and Economic Sciences at the National Science Foundation. She has served on many committees of the National Academies of Sciences, Engineering, and Medicine. She has a Ph.D. in sociology from Stanford University.

Susan E. Cozzens is professor emeritus of public policy at the Georgia Institute of Technology, where she previously served as director of the Technology Policy and Assessment Center and associate dean for research in the Ivan Allen College. She also previously served as director of the Office of Policy Support at the National Science Foundation (NSF) where she coordinated policy and management initiatives for the NSF director, primarily in peer review, strategic planning, and assessment. Her research interests are in science, technology, and innovation policies in developing countries, including issues of equity, equality, and development. She is active internationally in developing methods for research assessment and science and technology indicators. Her service on committees of the National Academies of Sciences, Engineering, and Medicine includes the Committee on Review of the Environmental Protection Agency's "Science to Achieve Results" Research Grants Program and the Committee on Evaluating the Efficiency of Research and Development Programs at the Environmental Protection Agency. She has a Ph.D. in sociology from Columbia University.

Barbara Entwisle is Kenan distinguished professor of sociology at the University of North Carolina at Chapel Hill, where she previously served as vice chancellor for research. She also previously served as director of the Carolina Population Center and as the center's training program director.

Her recent research includes examining the demographic responses to rapid social change, migration and social networks, and the interrelationships between population and environment in Northeast Thailand. She has been involved in the design and implementation of innovative social surveys around the world, including Add Health, the China Health and Nutrition Survey, the Russia Longitudinal Monitoring Survey, and the Nang Rong Surveys. She has served on several committees of the National Academies of Sciences, Engineering, and Medicine, including most recently as chair of the Standing Committee on the Future of Major NSF-Funded Social Science Surveys. She has a Ph.D. in sociology from Brown University.

Ivy Estabrooke is vice president of Corporate Executive Programs and Government Project Systems at PolarityTE, Inc. Previously, she was executive director of the Utah Science Technology and Research Initiative, and she served as the program officer for basic research in the Expeditionary Maneuver Warfare & Combating Terrorism Department at the Office of Naval Research (ONR). While at ONR, she managed a high-risk/high-payoff research portfolio including cutting-edge social and computational science programs and innovative neuroscience programs. She has also developed and implemented a strategy for examining emerging technology areas globally. At the National Academies of Sciences, Engineering, and Medicine, she served on the Committee on the Value of Social and Behavioral Science to National Priorities, among others. She has an M.S. in national security strategy and resource management from the Eisenhower School of the National Defense University and a Ph.D. in neuroscience from Georgetown University.

Paul A. Gade retired as a senior research psychologist and the chief of the Basic Research Unit of the U.S. Army Research Institute for the Behavioral and Social Sciences (ARI), where he developed and led ARI's intramural and extramural basic research programs. He currently holds a research professor appointment in the organizational sciences and communications department at George Washington University, where his work is focused on the history of ARI. His professional work covers military psychology history, theories and applications of intelligence and individual differences, and the neuroscience of how the brain generates the mind. His current research is on the history of military psychology. He is a fellow of the American Psychological Association (APA). He is also past president of the APA Society for Military Psychology and its and current historian. He received the Society's Charles S. Gersoni award for outstanding contributions to military psychology. He has a Ph.D. in experimental psychology from Ohio University.

Robert M. Hauser is the executive officer of the American Philosophical Society and the Vilas research professor and Samuel Stouffer professor of sociology, emeritus, at the University of Wisconsin–Madison. Formerly, he served as executive director of the Division of Behavioral and Social Sciences and Education at the National Academies of Sciences, Engineering, and Medicine. His research interests include statistical methodology, trends in social mobility and in educational progression and achievement, the uses of educational assessment as a policy tool, and changes in socioeconomic standing, cognition, health, and well-being across the life course. Previously, at the University of Wisconsin–Madison, he directed the Center for Demography and Ecology, the Center for Demography of Health and Aging, and the Institute for Research on Poverty. He is a member of the National Academy of Sciences, the American Academy of Arts and Sciences, the National Academy of Education, and the American Philosophical Society. He has a Ph.D. in sociology from the University of Michigan.

Steven G. Heeringa is a senior research scientist at the University of Michigan Institute for Social Research and a member of the faculty of the university's Program in Survey Methods and the Joint Program in Survey Methodology. Previously, he was the University of Michigan principal investigator for the multicenter Army STARRS study of suicide and adverse mental health outcomes in U.S. Army soldiers. He has served as a sample design consultant to international research programs in more than 30 countries worldwide, including Russia, the Ukraine, Uzbekistan, Kazakhstan, India, Nepal, China, Egypt, Iran, the United Arab Emirates, Qatar, South Africa, and Chile. He is a fellow of the American Statistical Association and an elected member of the International Statistical Institute. His service at the National Academies of Sciences, Engineering, and Medicine includes membership on the Committee to Evaluate the Department of Veterans Affairs Mental Health Services. He has a Ph.D. in biostatistics from the University of Michigan.

Daniel R. Ilgen is John A. Hannah distinguished professor of psychology and management at Michigan State University. He previously held faculty appointments at the University of Illinois at Urbana-Champaign, the U.S. Military Academy, West Point, and Purdue University. His research is in the areas of work motivation, team behavior, and leadership. He a fellow of the Association for Psychological Science, the American Psychological Association, the Academy of Management, the International Association of Applied Psychology, and the Society for Industrial and Organizational Psychology. He received the Distinguished Scientific Contributions Award from the Society of Industrial and Organizational Psychology and the Herbert A. Henneman, Jr. Lifetime Career Achievement Award from the Human Resources Division of the Academy of Management. He has served in numerous roles for the National Academies of Sciences, Engineering, and Medicine, including as a member of the Board on Behavioral, Cognitive, and Sensory Sciences. He has a Ph.D. in psychology from the University of Illinois.

Virginia Lesser is director of the Survey Research Center and department chair and professor in the department of statistics at Oregon State University. Her expertise includes survey methodology, applied statistics, environmental statistics, and ecological monitoring. She is a fellow of the American Statistical Association and an elected member of the International Statistical Institute. She has served on numerous committees of the National Academies of Sciences, Engineering, and Medicine, including the Committee on Capitalizing on Science, Technology, and Innovation: An Assessment of the Small Business Innovation Research Program-Phase II and the Committee on the Review of the National Institute of Safety and Health/Bureau of Labor Statistics Respirator Use Survey Program. She has a Ph.D. in biostatistics from the University of North Carolina at Chapel Hill.

Arthur Lupia is the Hal R. Varian professor of political science and research professor at the Institute for Social Research at the University of Michigan. His research explores how information and institutions affect policy and politics with a focus on how people make decisions when they lack information. He also works on issues related to data access and research transparency, and the value of social science and political science. He is the recipient of many honors and awards, including the Ithiel de Sola Pool Award from the American Political Science Association, the Warren Mitovsky Innovators Award from the American Association of Public Opinion Research, and the Award for Initiatives in Research of the National Academies of Sciences, Engineering, and Medicine. He is an elected fellow of the American Association for the Advancement of Science and an elected member of the American Academy of Arts and Sciences, and he is chair of the board at the Center for Open Science. He has a Ph.D. in political science from the California Institute of Technology.

Krisztina Marton (*Study Director*) is a senior program officer with the National Academies of Sciences, Engineering, and Medicine. She has directed many studies at the National Academies, including most recently the Panel to Evaluate the National Center for Science and Engineering Statistics Approach to Measuring the Science and Engineering Workforce. Prior to joining the National Academies staff, she was a survey researcher at Mathematica Policy Research where she conducted methodological research and oversaw data collections for the National Science Foundation, the Department of Health and Human Services, the Agency for Healthcare

Research and Quality, the Robert Wood Johnson Foundation, and other clients. Previously, she was a survey director in the The Ohio State University Center for Survey Research. She has a Ph.D. in communication with an interdisciplinary specialization in survey research from The Ohio State University.

Kathryn E. Newcomer is professor of public policy and public administration and former director of the Trachtenberg School of Public Policy and Public Administration at George Washington University. She frequently conducts research and training for federal and local government agencies and nonprofit organizations on performance measurement and program evaluation, and she has designed and conducted evaluations for several federal agencies and dozens of nonprofit organizations. She has served on many committees of the National Academies of Sciences, Engineering, and Medicine, including the Committee on Review of Specialized Degree-Granting Graduate Programs of the DoD in Science, Technology, Engineering, Mathematics (STEM) and Management and the Committee on Laboratory Security and Personnel Assurance Systems for Laboratories Conducting Research on Biological Select Agents and Toxins. She has a Ph.D. in political science from the University of Iowa.

Jeanne C. Rivard (*Senior Program Officer*) has worked on many studies at the National Academies of Sciences, Engineering, and Medicine, including serving as director of a study on proposed changes to federal regulations for protecting human participants in research and as co-director of a study on the evaluation of the National Institute on Disability and Rehabilitation Research and its grantees. She also worked on two studies for the Substance Abuse and Mental Health Services Administration; one on the science of changing behavioral health social norms and the other on behavioral health measurement. Prior to joining the National Academies, she was with the National Association of State Mental Health Program Directors Research Institute in Alexandria, Virginia, and on the faculty of the Columbia University School of Social Work in New York City. She has a master's degree from the University of South Carolina and a Ph.D. from the University of North Carolina at Chapel Hill, both in social work.

Adrienne Stith Butler is Associate Board Director of the Board on Behavioral, Cognitive, and Sensory Sciences at the National Academies of Sciences, Engineering, and Medicine. She has served as the study director for a wide range of National Academies studies, including projects on ending discrimination among people with mental and substance use disorders and on psychosocial interventions for mental and substance use disorders: a framework for establishing evidence-based standards. Prior to her work at the National

Academies, she was the James Marshall Public Policy Scholar, a fellowship sponsored by the American Psychological Association and the Society for the Psychological Study of Social Issues. She is a clinical psychologist and has a doctorate from the University of Vermont. She completed postdoctoral fellowships in adolescent medicine and pediatric psychology at the University of Rochester Medical Center.

Mark L. Weiss retired as the director of the Behavioral and Cognitive Sciences Division of the Directorate for Social, Behavioral and Economic Sciences at the National Science Foundation (NSF). Earlier at NSF he served as senior science adviser and as deputy assistant director of the directorate. Previously, he served as assistant director for Social, Behavioral and Economic Sciences at the Office of Science and Technology Policy in the Executive Office of the President, and he was professor and chair of the Department of Anthropology at Wayne State University. His research focuses on the application of genetic approaches to the study of nonhuman primate evolution and behavior. During his career he served on several interagency groups, including as NSF's representative to the White House's Committee on Sciences' Subcommittee on Forensic Science. He has a Ph.D. in physical anthropology from the University of California, Berkeley.